Integrated Auditing of ERP Systems

Integrated Auditing of ERP Systems

Yusufali F. Musaji

John Wiley & Sons, Inc.

Library of Congress Cataloging-in-Publication Data:

Musaji, Yasufali F.
 Integrated auditing of ERP systems / by Yusufali F. Musaji.
  p. cm.
 ISBN 0-471-23518-0 (cloth : alk. paper)
 1. Business--Data processing--Auditing. I. Title.
 HF5548.35.M87 2002
 657'.45--dc21

Printed in the United States of America.

10 9 8 7 6 5 4 3 2 1

Contents

Contents

Preface

This book is designed not to provide detailed audit/review programs for ERP systems but to underline the main concepts involved in each major phase of the ERP life cycle, as well as the major components of ERP systems of special interest to auditors. It is intended to familiarize the reader with the built-in controls in the ERP architecture and recommend control procedures which may have audit significance. It also offers useful advice to IS auditors and IT departments in systems and control design to move toward the integrated audit Approach.

Although this book is written for use within the audit function, it may also be of wider interest. Management may find the information useful in assessing the effectiveness of control procedures over systems at various points in their ERP life cycle stages. Audit can use the knowledge and know-how (gained as a reference) in designing their audit programs to evaluate and test controls over their ERP system.

Finally, this book will be helpful as a basis for developing training courses for general audit staff, IT audit specialists, internal auditors, and others. The necessity of providing training and practical IT audit experience to all levels of audit staff will continue to be the cornerstone of any integrated initiative. An increase in importance will continue as the availability of smaller, faster, less expensive computer systems contributes to the expanded use of computers in large and small businesses.

Integrated Auditing of ERP Systems

1

ERP System Implementation Overview

Never put off until tomorrow what you can do the day after tomorrow
—Mark Twain

INTRODUCTION

Enterprise Resource Planning (ERP) System implementation is both an art and science that consists of planning, implementation, and ongoing maintenance. This methodology is designed to automate the drudgery of implementation and provide organized approaches to problem solving by listing, diagramming, and documenting all steps. Structured methodologies help to standardize and systemize ERP implementation and maintenance by approaching them as an engineering discipline rather than as whims of individual software developers. It is essential to understand structured methodologies in the implementation of ERP systems.

The basic steps of structured methodologies are:

- *Project Definition and Requirement Analysis.* Defining the terms of reference, determining user needs and system constraints, generating a functional specification and a logical model for the best solutions.
- *External Design.* Detailing the design for a selected solution, including diagrams relating all programs, subroutines, and data flow.

1

- *Internal Design.*   Building, testing, installing, and tuning software.
- *Pre-implementation.*   Evaluation and acceptance
- *Implementation.*   Implementing systems.
- *Post-implementation.*   Evaluation of controls and debugging.

This book covers ERP systems, their life cycles, and their major components to aid in understanding of any major ERP, irrespective of brand. It discusses each phase in the ERP life cycle, including the roles of each principal participant, key activities, and deliverables. Particular attention is paid to the audit role, which is the primary focus in succeeding chapters and may have to be adjusted if the other participants in the process do not perform their roles adequately.

When an organization purchases an ERP system, the intent is that the purchased ERP system provides specific functions and benefits. These functions and benefits need to be articulated to ensure that the ERP system performs as desired. This process is called conducting a feasibility analysis. The purpose of the feasibility study is to provide:

- An analysis of the objectives, requirements, and system concepts.
- An evaluation of different approaches for reasonably achieving the objectives.
- Identification of a proposed approach.

The feasibility analysis normally covers:

- *Current working practices.*   These are examined in depth, revealing areas in the business where there is duplication of effort, or where procedures instituted in the distant past are carried out even though there is no longer any need for them.
- *Channels of information.*   These are examined because the feasibility study is concerned primarily with the input and output information of each internal system. Such a study ignores departmental boundaries and prejudices. When the true information patterns within a business are exposed, it is often possible to reorganize resources so that all relevant data is captured at the point where it can be used for decision.

- *Alternative approaches.* Alternative methods of handling or presenting the data should be considered.

- *Cost factors.* These must be clearly identified and show definite cost savings or related benefits. Existing costs must be examined and used as a basis for comparison. Since this presentation is likely to be related to the information structure rather than to the departmental organization, the new approach may suggest possible improvements that were hidden under the existing system.

- *Supporting services offered.* The training and the systems and programming assistance that will be available during the installation period.

- *Range compatibility.* If the workload expands, can the configuration be increased in power without extensive reprogramming?

Differences and similarities between traditional auditing (i.e., financial, operational and IT auditing) and how they may be integrated in a computerized environment will be discussed. Appropriate ERP/IT control objectives will be defined and correlated as criteria in the ERP system audit.

Integrated Auditing

The term *integrated auditing* came from the IT terminology *integrated data* that then gave rise to the process of Integrated Systems and Systems Integration Processes from which ERP systems emerged. An ERP product can be defined as one that helps automate a company's business process by employing an integrated user interface, an integrated data set, and an integrated code set. So, from a purely business perspective, it is in the auditor's interest to become completely integrated in order to keep pace with technology improvements.

Prior to ERP systems, companies stored important business records in many different departments. Departments used different systems and techniques to manage that information. Information might also have been duplicated many times within an organization without necessarily being identical or similarly up to date. Some of this information might only have been on paper, making it difficult to access across the organization. For example, a customer might call sales to inquire about the progress of an important order. Instead of answering the question by referring to a shared database, the sales rep would be forced to track down the order by making multiple calls to the company's manufacturing or shipping departments.

In a manufacturing firm, data relating to a product is typically kept by many different departments in the organization:

- A record showing product inventory balance is kept by the Inventory Control Department.
- Its cost and/or standard cost is shown on a record in the Cost Department.
- A record kept by the incentives department shows bonus percentages to be paid to employees for given levels of production.
- In the Finance/Accounting Department, a record of inventory values is kept for manufacturing account purposes.
- Shipping and Receiving maintains records of quantities shipped to customers and receipts of raw material.
- Returns keeps records of inventory returned.
- And the list goes on.

ERP systems originated to serve the information needs of manufacturing companies. Over time they have grown to serve other industries, including health care, financial services, the aerospace industry, and the consumer goods sector. With this growth, ERP systems, which first ran on mainframes before migrating to client/server systems, are now migrating to the Web and include numerous applications.

A vital business objective of ERP systems is to enable each department to know what is happening in the manufacturing plants and to get appropriate data in order to keep records up to date.

The first main characteristic of integrated systems is that they combine separate records relating to the same subject into one related record held in the computer. The new product record contains all items of relevant data that were previously kept in six or more separate records. You can visualize the challenges (i.e., security, confidentiality, accuracy, completeness, and reliability) that this record poses to all the separate departments.

The second feature of integrated systems is that the process of multirecording and transcribing data to update separate records is now replaced by one single input to the computer record. Therefore multi-inputs relating to transactions affecting the product are replaced by one single input to the product record held in the computer. Again, imagine the challenges or controls required to facilitate timely coordination and scheduling of all the processes (manual or otherwise) to be undertaken by the different departments so that the single input to the computer system, also referred to as the single point of entry, is accomplished.

By the preparation of suitable computer programs (e.g., software, applications, utilities, or combinations thereof) all the information needed by the separate departments can be produced when required. This is accomplished by processing the integrated records held on the Product MasterFile or in the Integrated Database. Integrated systems thus link together systems that traditionally have been kept separate and, by their very nature, cut across the conventional departmental boundaries that normally exist in a business.

The unified nature of an ERP system can lead to significant benefits, including fewer errors, improved speed and efficiency, and more complete access to information. With better access to information, employees and managers can gain a better understanding of what is going on in the enterprise so they make better business decisions. For example, an ERP system could let buyers in the Purchasing Department quickly adjust material orders when they see an increase or decrease in customer orders. The result? They will either ensure that orders are met on a timely basis or save on inventory expenses.

With this knowledge, what questions would you ask operational auditors, financial auditors, and IT auditors during the planning and execution of audit engagements?

Integrated auditing should ensure that controls are not duplicated. Effective controls in one department do not result in inefficient controls in another department. The overall objective of controls is to ensure that there is optimal time to market the product. Auditors should promote the enhancement of controls by being able to effectively communicate with each other.

Implementing ERP on platforms is not always easy because of the massive re-engineering process that involves security, quality assurance, and training for members of the organization entrusted to use the ERP systems. In addition to maximizing the operational effectiveness of

At this point, the ERP and the computing environment on which the ERP system operates have been treated separately. In reality, they are not mutually exclusive and independent. The strength of one affects the other. The focus of this book is on ERP systems. Our basis assumes a large networked system which stores, processes, and transmits sensitive data and information.

Enterprise Resource Planning (ERP) is an industry term for the broad set of activities supported by multimodule application software that helps a manufacturer or other business manage the important parts of its business, including product planning, parts purchasing, maintaining inventories, interacting with suppliers, providing customer service, and tracking orders. ERP can also include application modules for the finance and human resources aspects of a business. Typically, an ERP system uses or is integrated with a relational database system. The deployment of an ERP system can involve considerable analysis of business process, employee retraining, and new work procedures.

Unlike legacy systems, which used flat files and traditional IBM Indexed Sequential Access Methods (ISAM) and Virtual Sequential Access Methods (VSAM) for storage of data and information, ERP systems are used with relational databases. A relational database is a collection of data items organized as a set of formally described tables from which data can be accessed or reassembled in many different ways without having to reorganize the database tables.

The standard user and application program interface to a relational database is the structured query language (SQL). SQL statements are used both for interactive queries for information from a relational database and for gathering data for reports.

In addition to being relatively easy to create and access, a relational database has the important advantage of being easy to extend. After the original database creation, a new data category can be added without requiring that all existing applications be modified.

A relational database is a set of tables containing data in predefined categories. Each table (which is sometimes called a relation) contains one or more data categories in columns. Each row contains a unique instance of data for the categories defined by the columns. For example, a typical business order entry database would include a table that described a customer with columns for name, address, phone number, and so on. Another table would describe an order with columns for product, customer, date, sales price, and so on. A user of the database could obtain a view that fits the user's needs. For example, a branch office manager might like a view or report on all customers that had bought products after a certain date. A financial service manager in the same company could, from the same tables, obtain a report on accounts that needed to be paid.

CHARACTERISTICS OF ERP SYSTEMS

When most people refer to the "core" ERP applications or "modules," they mean the back-office capabilities to manage human resources, accounting and finance, manufacturing, and project-management functions. However, major ERP suites from Oracle, PeopleSoft, and SAP now provide much more—including modules for sales force automation, business intelligence, customer relationship management, and supply chain management.

Although the objectives of our review, evaluation, and testing of the control framework are the same, there are some significant differences between ERP and non-ERP systems. These differences are:

- In ERP systems, certain control procedures leave no documentary evidence of performance. For some other procedures, the evidence of performance is indirect; it may be included in the program logic or in the operator's instructions. Therefore, compliance tests may have to be structured differently in an ERP environment and observation of the client's procedures may become more important.

- In ERP systems, information is often recorded in a form that cannot be read without the use of a computer.

- Financial and business information is often generated automatically by ERP systems based on data previously entered, without further human instructions.

- Errors that might be observed in non-ERP systems may go undetected because of the reduced human involvement in computerized processing. There is a danger that errors in processing may be applied to a large number of transactions without being noticed.

- With proper controls, ERP systems can be more reliable than non-ERP systems. This is because ERP systems subject all data to the same procedures and controls. Non-ERP systems are subject to random human error. Although computer processing will usually be consistent, errors may still occur; for example, if the computer is incorrectly programmed.

- It is difficult to make changes after an ERP system has been implemented. Therefore, we should be aware of the organization's plans to introduce significant new systems or to make major modifications to existing systems. It is advisable to review new systems or modifications before implementation so that a preliminary assessment can be made of the adequacy of control procedures, in order to ensure an adequate audit trail, and to plan any necessary changes in the audit approach.

ERP systems vary from the simplest, batch-controlled type to complex integrated applications that perform a number of functions simultaneously.

Batch-Controlled Systems

In a computer, a batch job is a program that is assigned to the computer to run without further user interaction. Examples of batch jobs in a PC are a printing request or an analysis of a web site log. In larger commercial computers or servers, batch jobs are usually initiated by a system user. Some are defined to run automatically at a certain time.

In some ERP systems, batch jobs run in the background and interactive programs run in the foreground. In general, interactive programs have priority over batch programs, which run during the time intervals when the interactive programs are waiting for user requests.

The term *batch job* originated when punched cards were the usual form of computer input and the computer operator fed a sequenced batch of cards into the computer. (Hopefully, the output came back the next morning.)

In a typical batch system, user departments periodically submit batches of transactions to the IT department for transcription and processing. Batch totals are normally developed manually, thus setting up control totals which can be reconciled through successive processing stages to the file update report or to the final printed output.

When computers were first introduced, the batch system was predominant. Now many organizations are moving toward the more advanced systems described below.

Online Systems

In computers, interactivity is the dialog that occurs between a human being (or possibly another live creature) and a computer program. (Programs that run without immediate user involvement are not interactive; they are usually called batch or background programs.) Games usually foster a great amount of interactivity. Order-entry applications and many other business applications are also interactive but in a more constrained way, offering fewer options for user interaction.

The World Wide Web offers not only interaction with the browser (the Web application program) but also with the pages that the browser brings up. The implicit invitations called hypertext link to other pages and provide the most common form of interactivity on the Web (which can be thought of as a giant, interconnected application program).

In addition to hypertext, the Web (and many non-Web applications in any computer system) offers other possibilities for interactivity. Any kind of user input, including typing commands or clicking the mouse, is a form of input. Displayed images and text, printouts, motion-video sequences, and sounds are output forms of interactivity.

The earliest form of interaction with computers was indirect, submitting commands on punched cards and letting the computer read and perform the commands. Later computer systems were designed so that average people (not just programmers) could interact immediately with computers, telling them what programs to run. People could interact with word processors (called editors), drawing programs, and other interactive programs. The first interactive human-computer interfaces were input-text sequences called "commands" (as in "DOS commands") and terse one-line responses from the system.

In the late 1970s, the first graphical-user interfaces (GUIs) emerged from the Xerox PARC Lab, found their way into the Apple Macintosh personal computer, and then into Microsoft's Windows operating systems and thus into almost all personal computers available today.

A GUI (usually pronounced GOO-ee) is a graphical-user interface (rather than purely textual user interface) to a computer. As you read this, you are looking at the GUI or graphical user interface of your particular Web browser. The term came into existence because the first interactive user interfaces to computers were not graphical; they were text-and-keyboard oriented and usually consisted of commands you had to remember and computer responses that were infamously brief. The command interface of the DOS operating system (which you can still get to from your Windows operating system) is an example of the typical user-computer interface before GUIs arrived. An intermediate step in user interfaces between the command-line interface and the GUI was the non-graphical, menu-based interface, which let you interact by using a mouse rather than by typing in keyboard commands.

Today's major operating systems provide a graphical-user interface. Applications typically use the elements of the GUI that come with the operating system and add their own graphical-user interface elements and ideas. A GUI sometimes uses metaphors for real-life objects, the desktop, the view through a window, or the physical layout in a building. Elements of a GUI include windows, pull-down menus, buttons, scroll bars, iconic images, wizards, the mouse, and, no doubt, many things that have not been invented yet. With the increasing use of multimedia, sound, voice, motion video, and virtual reality interfaces are likely to become part of the GUI for many applications. A system's graphical-user interface along with its input devices is sometimes referred to as its "look-and-feel."

Online processing permits direct entry of transactions into the computer by user departments, frequently without batch controls. These systems permit the use of controls, such as automatic editing procedures, which can be more effective and instantaneous than batch controls.

There are many varieties of online systems, but they can be divided into three main groups:

- *Online inquiry, with batch-controlled data entry for transactions, master files and databases.*

  In this approach, the operator at an online terminal can access stored data and learn the status of an account or transaction as of the last update, but cannot change the records. For example, in an order processing system, the credit manager may be able to access customer accounts and find out their current balance, but the computer files can be updated only by using batch processing. In this situation, our review of internal controls should concentrate on the controls over batch processing.

Although not online, remote job entry (RJE) systems have control implications similar to online systems with batch-controlled data entry. RJE systems use remote facilities for entering batch-processing jobs into a computer from magnetic tape, or magnetic disk. For example, the operator may enter shipping documents together with batch-control information. The program reconciles the batch-control information and prints a message that indicates whether the shipping documents entered are in balance with the control information.

- *Online inquiry, with online data entry, data validation, and data collection. Master file updating from transaction files (online data capture).*

In this case, individual transactions are entered through remote terminals and transmitted to a central computer where they are edited and validated; and, if accepted, stored in a transaction or daybook file. Later, normally overnight, the transaction file is used to update the master records. The user at the remote terminal has no capability to change the master records directly. These systems should be controlled in a manner similar to batch systems, with input totals accumulated and reconciled with totals calculated by the computer.

- *Online inquiry with online updating of both transaction and master files (real time update).*

The most complex system to design and control is a real time update system. In these systems, the operator uses the terminal to update the master files directly by entering one transaction at a time. The computer file is said to be "transaction driven." In such a system, there may be few user-input controls. Extensive programmed edit and logging controls are required to protect the computer files from erroneous or unauthorized transactions. It is also essential for important printed reports, such as control reports, exception reports, or summaries, to be carefully reviewed by a user department employee who is not responsible for entering transactions.

Online Systems Problems

Problems relating to online systems include:

- Data may be lost or altered during transmission of transactions from the user terminal to the computer.
- Many employees may be able to enter transactions through the terminals, thereby increasing the opportunity for erroneous or unauthorized entries.
- Additional procedures may be needed to handle processing malfunctions. The IT department must be able to identify what transactions have and have not been processed. It must be possible to return to a known position (checkpoint) and reprocess transactions from that checkpoint.

Distributed Data Processing

Distributed data processing refers to a network of local computers or minicomputers that are often online to a central computer installation. Typical systems are:

- Local editing of input; primary processing at the central computer; online inquiries to the central computer.
- Local editing of input; processing at the local computer and the central computer; online inquiries to both the local and central computers.
- Local editing of input; primary processing at the local computer on the local master file; consolidation of financial and business data from the local master file at the central computer; online inquiries to the local computer.
- Local editing; processing and file updates by a network of linked computers with no central computer installation.

An important feature of distributed data processing systems is that internal control may be divided among several physical locations or levels of processing. For example, in some systems, local personnel can modify the programs used by the local computers. In other cases the programs are controlled and can be modified only by personnel at the central computer installation.

Integrated Systems

Data processing is integrated when either input or generated data automatically updates the data files used in more than one system. A common example is the input of a customer sales order that automatically generates shipping documents, priced sales invoices, inventory issue instructions, and all related ledger postings.

Where conventional batch-processing systems are integrated, the successive processing steps will be executed by separate subsystems (program suites) in a logical order with batched data being progressively transferred from one program to the next. In these systems, we can usually expect to find a visible trail of "run-to-run" controls which can be reconciled to the original input batch totals. In such systems, it is unusual to find any significant loss of audit trail regarding the control totals, but there may be difficulties in identifying the individual items included in those totals.

In transaction driven systems, however, data files belonging to more than one application may be updated simultaneously by each individual item. For example, a sales transaction may update both account receivable and inventory records. In such systems traditional run-to-run controls do not exist and the potential for loss of audit trail is significant.

Databases

A database is a collection of data used by several different applications. It may be accessed using conventional access methods, or it may be organized and accessed by a database management system (DBMS). The DBMS is normally standard software supplied by either the computer manufacturer or by a software house.

When using a database management system, the data is independent of the application programs. The structure of the data comprising the whole database is defined by the DBMS. This structure is generally referred to as a "schema." Each individual application program will usually concern itself only with part of the total schema. The application program's view of the database is called its "sub-schema."

When there is sharing of data among many users, the responsibility for the accuracy of the data must be clearly established. This is often done through the database administrator (DBA), who should be independent of both users and programmers (Key Control Consideration).

The DBA should establish and update a data dictionary/directory system. The dictionary/directory should be concerned with the contents of the database and rules for its updating. In some cases, it is a manual document; in others, computerized. It is a major control tool for management and audit, providing, in effect, a map of information relating to database processing.

Rigorous edit and validation checks should be applied to input data. Since several programs use a data element, a single error may have multiple effect. This is known as "cascading" or "cumulative" error.

Automatic recovery and restart procedures are included in most Database Management Systems (DBMS). Recovery procedures are designed to prevent the loss of the database and of transactions being processed, whereas restart procedures relate to the resumption of computer processing.

Few people would have thought of enterprise resource planning (ERP) in terms of rapid change. ERP systems have been around since the mid-1970s when they first ran on mainframe computers. Enterprises that invested huge sums in these big and complex systems now have elaborate legacy setups that they absolutely depend on to run their companies. Because there is so much at stake, ERP providers and customers introduce changes to technology and deployments gradually to avoid costly mistakes.

Nonetheless, ERP systems *do* change—albeit slowly. People started talking about adapting ERP software to client/server technology at the beginning of the 1980s, but it was not until the late 1990s that more client/server versions shipped than mainframe versions.

Today, ERP is still evolving, adapting to developments in technology and the demands of the market. Four important trends are shaping ERP's continuing evolution: improvements in integration and flexibility; extensions to e-business applications, a broader reach to new users; and the adoption of Internet technologies. Taking a closer look at each will help you understand where ERP is headed.

2

ERP System Vulnerabilities and Controls

NEED FOR AN ERP RISK ASSESSMENT

ERPs have substantially altered the method by which administrative processes, such as payroll, accounts payable, inventory, sales and accounts receivable, operate, are controlled and audited. Opportunities for personal review and clerical checking have declined as the collection and subsequent uses of data have changed. The changes are the result of moving from manual procedures performed by individuals familiar with both the data and the accounting process; to high volume, automated processes performed by individuals unfamiliar with either the data or the accounting practices.

Information Technology has substantially reduced the time available for the review of transactions before their entry into the automated system's records. In poorly controlled systems the opportunity for discovering errors or fraud before they have an impact on operations is reduced, especially in the case of real time, distributed, and database systems. The radical growth of these system configurations (or architectures) has increased the importance of both automated and manual internal control/security procedures. It is imperative, therefore, that these systems are reviewed, as they are being implemented; to ensure that adequate controls and security are designed into the ERP system from the outset.

IMPLEMENTATION VERSUS OPERATIONAL AUDIT

Auditing in an ERP environment can be divided into two broad areas. First is the audit of ERP systems under implementation and second is the audit of operational ERP systems. These two types of audits require significantly different approaches.

In an implementation (vanilla or otherwise) of an ERP system, there is no operational system or output data. The auditor evaluates controls without the benefit of observing processing results. In an implementation audit, the auditor is concerned with ensuring that the implementation procedures and standards have been properly followed.

The audit of operational ERP systems evaluates the results of the automated processes. It is normally a data-oriented audit, looking at processed transactions. The adequacy and effectiveness of the system controls can be evaluated by examining the results of operation (i.e., did the application produce the anticipated outcome).

The operational audits can identify vulnerabilities, but these are costly to correct after implementation because of the associated costs (in money and operational downtime). Studies have shown that it costs approximately 50–100 times more to correct an operational system than it would have cost to build in the necessary controls during implementation. Indeed, the cost to retrofit controls into a system increases geometrically as one progress through the ERP system life cycle phases.

If potential vulnerabilities can be identified during implementation of ERP systems, they can be more easily and economically corrected than after the ERP system is installed and operational. Thus, it becomes imperative to evaluate the adequacy of the implementation approach to controls (i.e., how controls are addressed, implemented, and documented). If an adequate system of controls is built in during implementation, it can be fine-tuned through operational audits, as necessary. The risks and exposures through the model ERP life cycle (ERPCL) are presented in Exhibits 3.1a–3.2e, which include the operational environment and maintenance phases.

OVERVIEW OF RISKS

Organizations assume risks in the normal conduct of doing business. These risks represent potential damaging events that might produce

Exhibit 2.1   Risks and exposures for ERPLC

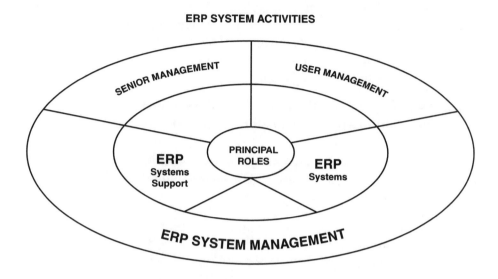

losses. Controls or safeguards are installed to reduce these risks. If controls are insufficient, the organization is overexposed and is likely to suffer losses or operate at a less efficient level than competitors.

Any IT environment presents unique vulnerabilities and threats to an organization. Vulnerability is a weakness or a flaw in an IT-based system that may be exploited by a threat that can cause destruction or by misuse of the system's assets or resources. Threats can be environmental (e.g., fire, water damage, earthquakes, hurricanes, etc.) or people-oriented (e.g., errors, omissions, intentional acts of violence, fraud, etc.). When a threat materializes and takes advantage of a system's vulnerabilities, a damaging event causes a loss. The risks of damaging events cannot be totally eliminated, but the use of controls can reduce such risks to an acceptable level.

Risk Analyses

A risk analysis of an organization's ERP systems, their existing controls, and their vulnerabilities results in the loss potential for the system, with an estimated likelihood of occurrence. This loss potential in damages must be represented in terms of dollar value.

A risk analysis of an ERP system performs two important functions:

1. Searches out an ERP system's vulnerabilities and the probabilities of threats materializing to exploit these vulnerabilities.
2. Calculates the damage or loss to its assets that could be produced by the resulting damaging events.

A third component, to recommend controls or safeguards that would reduce the damages or loss to an acceptable level (through the use of a cost/benefit analysis), might also be added.

An ERP system environment's vulnerabilities and set of threats should be assessed to arrive at some estimate of possible damaging events. Such an assessment would also review the strengths of existing controls.

A vulnerability assessment is conducted as part of a risk analysis. The vulnerability assessment is a major assessment of the adequacy of an ERP's system. Organizations must first identify vulnerabilities and threats; and then determine whether controls are adequate to reduce the resulting risks to an acceptable level. If not, it will be necessary to correct and guard against threats.

RISKS IN AN ERP ENVIRONMENT

The risks in an ERP environment include both those present in a manual processing environment and those that are unique or increased in an ERP environment. The use of ERP systems clearly introduces additional risks into the system environment. These additional risks include problems associated with:

- Improper use of technology.
- Inability to control technology.
- Inability to translate user needs into technical requirements.
- Illogical processing.

- Inability to react quickly (to stop processing).
- Cascading of errors.
- Repetition of errors.
- Incorrect entry of data.
- Concentration of data.
- Inability to substantiate processing.
- Concentration of responsibilities.

Each of these risks is discussed individually below, including many of the conditions that cause the risks to occur.

Improper Use of Technology

Information technology provides systems analysts and programmers with a variety of processing capabilities. This technology must be matched to the user's needs in order to best meet those needs. A mismatch of technology and needs can result in an unnecessary expenditure of organizational resources.

One of the more common misuses of technology is the introduction of new technology prior to the clear establishment of its need. For example, many organizations introduce database technology without clearly establishing the need for that technology. Experience has shown that the early users of a new technology frequently consume large amounts of resources learning to use that new technology.

The conditions that lead to the improper use of technology include:

- Premature user of new hardware technology.
- Early user of new software technology.
- Minimal planning for the installation of new hardware and software technology.
- Systems analyst/programmer improperly skilled in the use of technology.

Inability to Control Technology

IT personnel spend most of their effort on the problems associated with the implementation of new technology. Numerous studies imply that there is often too little time left to develop and install technological controls. As a result, resources are expended to correct technological problems.

Controls are needed over the technological environment. These controls ensure that the proper version of the proper program is in production at the right time; that the proper files are mounted; and that the operators perform the proper instructions. Adequate procedures must be developed to prevent, detect, and correct problems in the operating environment. The proper data must be maintained and retrievable when needed. The conditions that result in uncontrolled technology include:

- Selection of vendor-offered system control capabilities by systems programmers without considering audit needs.
- Too many control trade-offs for operational efficiency.
- Inadequate restart/recovery procedures.
- Inadequate control over different versions of programs.
- Inadequate control over schedulers, system operators, tape librarians, print capabilities, and data transmission capabilities.
- Inadequate review of outputs.

Inability to Translate User Needs into Technical Requirements

One of the major failures of information technology has been a communication failure between users and technical personnel. In many organizations, users cannot adequately express their needs in terms that facilitate the implementation of ERP applications. And the technical people are often unable to appreciate the concerns and requirements of their users.

The risk associated with failure to satisfy user needs is complex. Exposures include:

- Failure to implement needs because users were unaware of technical capabilities.
- Improperly implemented needs because the technical personnel did not understand user requirements.
- Users accepting improperly implemented needs because they are unsure how to specify changes.

- Building of redundant manual systems to compensate for weaknesses in ERP applications.

Conditions that can lead to the inability to translate user needs into technical requirements include:

- Users without technical IT skills.
- Technical people without sufficient understanding of user requirements.
- User's inability to specify requirements in sufficient detail.
- Multi-user systems with no user in charge of the system.

Illogical Processing

Illogical processing is the performance of an automated event that would be highly unlikely in a manual processing environment; for example, producing a payroll check for a clerical individual for over $1 million. This is possible in an automated system due to programming or hardware errors, but highly unlikely in a manual system.

ERP applications do not have the same human oversight as manual systems. In addition, fewer people have a good understanding of the processing logic of ERP applications. Thus, in some instances, illogical processing may not be readily recognizable.

Conditions that can result in illogical processing include:

- Failure to check for unusually large amounts on output documents.
- Fields that are either too small or too large, thereby impacting the completeness, accuracy, or efficiency of the data being processed.
- Failure to scan output documents.

Inability to React Quickly

ERP applications are valuable because they are able to satisfy user needs on a timely basis. Some of these needs are predetermined and reports are prepared on a regular basis to meet these needs. Other needs occur periodically and require special actions to satisfy. If the ERP application is unable to satisfy these special needs on a timely basis, redundant systems may be built for that purpose.

One of the measures of an ERP application's success is the speed with which special requests can be satisfied. Some of the newer online database applications that include a query language can satisfy some requests within a very short time span. On the other hand, some of the older batch-oriented applications may take several days or weeks to satisfy a special request. In some instances, the structure of the application system is an inhibits satisfying requests. For example, if an auditor wants all of the supporting information for a supply requisition in a tape-batched system, the cost and difficulty of satisfying that request may be prohibitive. That requisition could be spread over many weeks of processing, due to back orders, returned shipments, and shipping errors. The evidence supporting the transaction may be spread over many tape files and the cost of processing those files may be exorbitant.

The conditions that make ERP applications unable to react quickly include:

- Computer time is unavailable to satisfy the request, or computer terminals/microcomputers are not readily accessible to users.
- The structure of the computer files is inconsistent with the information requested.
- General-purpose extract programs are not available to satisfy the desired request.
- The cost of processing exceeds the value of the information requested.

Cascading of Errors

Cascading of errors is the domino effect of errors throughout an application system. An error in one part of the program or application triggers a second yet unrelated error in another part of the application system. This second error may trigger a third error, and so on.

The cascading of error *risk* is frequently associated with making changes to application systems. A change is made and tested in the program in which the change occurs. However, some condition has been altered as a result of the change, which causes an error to occur in another part of the application system.

Cascading of errors can occur between applications. *This risk intensifies as applications become more integrated.* For example, a system that is accepting orders may be tied through a series of applications to a system that replenishes inventory based upon orders. Thus, an insignificant error in the order-entry program can "cascade" through a series of applications resulting in a very serious error in the inventory replenishment program.

The types of conditions that lead to cascading of errors include:

- Inadequately tested applications.
- Failure to communicate the type and date of changes being implemented.
- Limited testing of program changes.

Repetition of Errors

In a manual processing environment, errors are made individually. Thus, a person might process one item correctly, make an error on the next, process the next twenty correctly, and then make another error. In ERP systems, the rules are applied consistently. Thus, if the rules are correct, processing is always correct. But, if the rules are erroneous, processing will always be erroneous.

Errors can result from application programs, hardware failures, and failures in vendor-supplied software. For example, a wrong percentage may have been entered for tax deductions. Thus, every employee for that pay period will have the wrong amount deducted for tax purposes.

The conditions that cause repetition of errors include:

- Insufficient program testing.
- Inadequate checks on entry of master information.
- Failure to monitor the results of processing.

Incorrect Entry of Data

In ERP applications, there is a mechanical step required to convert input data into machine-readable format. In the process of conducting this task, errors can occur. Data that was properly prepared and authorized may be entered into ERP applications incorrectly.

Much of the data entered into batch-type systems is entered using a keyboard device. Some of these devices are keypunch machines and key-to-disk machines. The data originator manually transcribes the input information onto some type of form, and the form is given to a key operator to enter on computer media. During this keying process, errors can be made.

In the newer technology, data can be originated and entered at the same time. For example, order entry clerks receive orders by telephone and key them directly into computer memory. However, errors can still occur during this process.

Other methods of data entry include optical scanners, process-control computers that monitor production machinery, automatic cash dispensers and point-of-sale equipment. However, these are all mechanical devices and thus subject to failure.

Conditions that can cause incorrect entry of data include:

- Human errors in keying data.
- Mechanical failure of hardware devices.
- Misinterpretation of characters or meaning of manually recorded input.
- Misunderstanding of data entry procedures.
- Inadequate data verification procedures.

Concentration of Data

ERP applications concentrate data in an easy-to-access format. In manual systems, data is voluminous and stored in many places. It is difficult for an unauthorized individual to spend much time browsing undetected through file cabinets or other manual storage areas.

With ERP media, unauthorized individuals can browse using computer programs. This may be difficult to detect without adequate safeguards. In addition, the data can be copied quickly without leaving any visible trail or destroying the original data. Thus, the owners of the data may not be aware that the data has been *compromised.*

Database technology increases the risk of data manipulation and compromise. The more data that is stored in a single place, the greater the value of that data to an unauthorized individual. For example, the information about an individual in the payroll application is restricted to current pay information. But, when that data is coupled with personnel history, not only current pay information, but also pay history, individual skills, years and progression of employment, and perhaps performance evaluation is available.

Concentration of data increases the problems of greater reliance on a single piece of data and reliance on a single file. If the data entered is erroneous, the more applications that rely on that piece of data, the greater the impact of the error. And the more applications that use the concentrated data, the greater the impact when that data is unavailable due to problems with the hardware or software used for processing it.

The conditions that can create problems due to the concentration of data in ERP applications include:

- Erroneous data and its impact on multiple users of that data.

- Impact of hardware and software failures that ordinarily make the data available to multiple users.

- Inadequate access controls enabling unauthorized access to data.

- Inefficient use of system for data storage and/or retrieval, which may impact response time or computer capacity.

Inability to Substantiate Processing

ERP applications should contain the capability to substantiate processing. This substantiation includes both the ability to reconstruct the processing of a single transaction and the ability to reconstruct control totals. ERP applications should be able to produce all of the source transactions that support a control total as well as substantiate that any source document is contained in a control total.

Application systems need to substantiate processing to correct errors and to prove that processing is correct. When errors occur, computer personnel need to pinpoint the cause so they can be corrected. ERP application customers, other users, and control-oriented personnel, such as auditors, frequently want to verify that processing is correct.

Conditions that may cause the inability to substantiate processing include:

- Evidence is not retained long enough.

- The evidence from intermediate processing is not retained.

- Evidence is not independently reviewed for quality assurance and/or data integrity.

- Outputs are not reviewed for quality by the users.
- The cost of substantiating processing exceeds the benefits derived from the process.

Concentration of Responsibilities

ERP systems concentrate the responsibilities of many people into the automated application. Responsibilities that had been divided among many people for control purposes may be concentrated into a single application system. A single application system may also concentrate responsibilities from many departments within an organization.

The responsibilities in an ERP environment may be concentrated in both the application system and IT personnel. For example, the database administrator may absorb data control responsibilities from many areas in the organization. A single ERP system project leader may have the processing responsibility for many areas in the organization. New methods of separation of duties must be substituted for the previous segregation of duties among people.

Conditions that cause the concentration of responsibilities in an ERP environment include:

- Establishment of a data processing programming and systems group to develop ERP applications for an organization.
- Centralized processing of ERP applications.
- Establishment of a database administration function.
- Lack of adequate standards and enforcement of those standards.
- Lack of adequate quality assurance and systems or applications testing.

The following is a list of negative situations to which ERP application systems are vulnerable, grouped according to common system organizational structures. While not intended to be all-inclusive, the list suggests various kinds of vulnerabilities that may exist in an ERP system. This list of potential vulnerabilities helps identify the additional risks presented in an ERP environment. Due to their value as a tool to identify unique risks, a brief description of vulnerabilities by type is also provided.

- *Erroneous or Falsified Data Input.*

  Erroneous or falsified input data is the simplest and most common cause of undesirable performance by an applications system. Vulnerabilities occur wherever data is collected, manually processed, or prepared for entry to the computer.

  - Unreasonable or inconsistent source data values may not be detected.
  - Keying errors during transcription may not be detected.
  - Incomplete or poorly formatted data records may be accepted as if they were complete records.
  - Records in one format may be interpreted according to a different format.
  - An employee may fraudulently add, delete, or modify data (e.g., payment vouchers, claims) to obtain benefits (e.g., checks, negotiable coupons) for himself.
  - Lack of document counts and other controls over source data or input transactions may allow some of the data or transactions to be lost without detection or allow extra records to be added.
  - Records about the data entry personnel (e.g., a record of a personnel action) may be modified during data entry.
  - Data that arrives at the last minute (or under some other special or emergency condition) may not be verified prior to processing.
  - Records in which errors have been detected may be corrected without verification of the full record.

- *Misuse by Authorized End Users.*

  End users are the people served by ERP Systems. The system is designed for their use, but they can also misuse it. It may be difficult to determine whether their use of the system is in accordance with the legitimate performance of their job.

  - An employee may convert confidential information to an unauthorized use. For example, he may sell privileged data about an individual to a prospective employer, credit agency, insurance company, or competitor; or may use statistics for stock market transactions before their public release.

- A user whose job requires access to individual records in a file may compile a complete listing of the file and then make unauthorized use of it (e.g., sell a listing of employee's home addresses as a mailing list).
- Information may be altered for an unauthorized end user (e.g., altering of personnel records).
- An authorized user may use the system for personal benefit (e.g., theft of services).
- A supervisor may manage to approve and enter a fraudulent transaction.
- A disgruntled or terminated employee may destroy or modify records, possibly in such a way that backup records are also corrupted and useless.
- An authorized user may accept a bribe to modify or obtain information.

- *Uncontrolled System Access.*

  Organizations expose themselves to unnecessary risk if they fail to establish controls over who can enter the system area, who can use the ERP and who can access the information contained in the system.

  - Data or programs may be stolen from the IT room or other storage areas.
  - ERP facilities may be destroyed or damaged by intruders or employees.
  - Individuals may not be adequately identified before they are allowed to enter the IT area.
  - Remote terminals may not be adequately protected from use by unauthorized persons.
  - An unauthorized user may gain access to the system via a dial-in line and an authorized user's password.
  - Passwords may be inadvertently revealed to unauthorized individuals. A user may write his password in some convenient place, or the password may be obtained from some other apparent source, discarded printouts, or by observing the user as he types it.

- A user may leave a logged-in terminal unattended, allowing an unauthorized person to use it.

- A terminated employee may retain access to an ERP system because his name and password are not immediately deleted from authorization tables and control lists.

- An unauthorized individual may gain access to the system for his own purposes (e.g., theft of computer services, data or programs, modification of data, alteration of programs, sabotage, denial of services).

- Repeated attempts by the same user or terminal to gain unauthorized access to the system or to a file may go undetected.

- *Ineffective Security Practices for the Application.*

  Inadequate manual checks and controls to ensure correct processing by the AIS, or negligence by those responsible for carrying out these checks, result in many vulnerabilities.

  - Poorly defined criteria for authorized access may cause employees not to know what information they, or others, are permitted to access.

  - The person responsible for security may fail to restrict user access to only those processes and data that are needed to accomplish assigned tasks.

  - Large funds disbursements, unusual price changes, and unanticipated inventory usage may not be reviewed for accuracy.

  - Repeated payments to the same party may go unnoticed because there is no review.

  - Sensitive data may be carelessly handled by the application staff, by the mail service, or by other personnel within the organization.

  - Post-processing reports analyzing system operations may not be reviewed to detect security violations.

  - Inadvertent modification or destruction of files may occur when trainees are allowed to work on live data.

  - Appropriate action may not be pursued when a security variance is reported to the system security officer or to the perpetrating individual's supervisor. In fact, procedures covering such occurences may not exist.

- *Procedural Errors within the IT Facility.*

  Both errors and intentional acts committed by the DP operations staff may result in improper operational procedures, lapsed controls, and losses in storage media and output.

- *Procedures and Controls.*

  ○ Files may be destroyed during database reorganization or during release of disk space.

  ○ Operators may ignore operational procedures; for example, by allowing programmers to operate computer equipment.

  ○ Job control language parameters may be erroneous.

  ○ An installation manager may circumvent operational controls to obtain information.

  ○ Careless or incorrect restarting after shutdown may cause the state of a transaction update to be unknown.

  ○ An operator may enter erroneous information at a CPU console (e.g., control switch in wrong position, terminal user allowed full system access; operator cancels wrong job from queue).

  ○ Hardware maintenance may be performed while production data is online and the equipment undergoing maintenance is not isolated.

  ○ An operator may perform unauthorized acts for personal gain (e.g., make extra copies of competitive bidding reports, print copies of unemployment checks; delete a record from a journal file).

  ○ Operations staff may sabotage the computer (e.g., drop pieces of metal into a terminal).

  ○ The wrong version of a program may be executed.

  ○ A program may be executed using wrong data or may be executed twice using the same transactions.

  ○ An operator may bypass required safety controls (e.g., write rings for tape reels).

- ○ Supervision of operations personnel may not be adequate during non-working-hour shifts.
- ○ Due to incorrectly learned procedures, an operator may alter or erase the master files.
- ○ A console operator may override a label check without recording the action in the security log.
- *Storage Media Handling.*
  - ○ Critical tape files may be mounted without being write protected.
  - ○ Inadvertently or intentionally mislabeled storage media are erased. In case they contain backup files, the erasure may not be noticed until it is needed.
  - ○ Internal labels on storage media may not be checked for accuracy.
  - ○ Files with missing or mislabeled expiration dates may be erased.
  - ○ Incorrect processing of data or erroneous updating of files may occur when input data has been dropped; partial input data is used; write rings mistakenly are placed in tapes; wrong tapes are incorrectly mounted or worn tapes mounted.
  - ○ Scratch tapes used for jobs processing sensitive data may not be adequately erased after use.
  - ○ Temporary files written during a job step for use in subsequent steps may be erroneously released or modified because they are not protected or because of an abnormal termination.
  - ○ Storage media containing sensitive information may not get adequate protection because operations staff does not know the nature of the information content.
  - ○ Tape management procedures may not adequately account for the current status of all tapes.
  - ○ Magnetic storage media that contain very sensitive information may not be degaussed before being released.
  - ○ Output may be sent to the wrong individual or terminal.

- ◦ Improper operation of output or post-processing units (e.g., bursters, decollators, or multipart forms) may result in loss of output.
- ◦ Surplus output material (e.g., duplicates of output data, used carbon paper) may not be disposed of properly.
- ◦ Tapes and programs that label output for distribution may be erroneous or not protected from tampering.

- *Program Errors.*

  ERP system should operate in an environment that requires and supports complete, correct, and consistent program design, good programming practices, adequate testing, review, documentation, and proper maintenance procedures. Although programs developed and implemented in such an environment may still contain undetected errors, programs not developed in this manner may be rife with errors. Without these controls, programmers can deliberately modify programs to produce undesirable side effects or they can misuse the programs they monitor.

  - ◦ Records may be deleted from sensitive files without a guarantee that the deleted records can be reconstructed.
  - ◦ Programmers may insert special provisions in programs that manipulate data concerning themselves (e.g., a payroll programmer may alter his own payroll records).
  - ◦ Data may not be stored separately from code so that program modifications are more difficult and must be made more frequently.
  - ◦ Program changes may not be tested adequately before being used in a production run.
  - ◦ Changes to a program may result in new errors due to unanticipated interactions between program modules.
  - ◦ Program acceptance tests may fail to detect errors that only occur for unusual combinations of input (e.g., a program that is supposed to reject all except a specified range of values actually accepts an additional value).
  - ◦ Programs with contents that should be safeguarded may not be identified and protected.

- Code, test data with its associated output, and documentation for certified programs may not be filed and retained for reference.
- Documentation for vital programs may not be safeguarded.
- Programmers may fail to keep a change log, to maintain back copies, or to formalize record-keeping activities.
- An employee may steal programs he maintains and use them for personal gain (e.g., sale to a commercial organization, hold another organization for extortion).
- A critical data value may be initialized twice due to poor program design. An error may occur when the program is modified to change the data value, but only changes it in one place.
- Production data may be disclosed or destroyed when it is used during testing.
- A programmer who misunderstands requests for changes to the program may cause errors.
- A programmer who makes changes directly to machine code may introduce errors.
- Programs may contain routines not compatible with their intended purposes, which can disable or bypass security protection mechanisms. For example, a programmer who anticipates being fired, inserts code into a program which will cause vital system files to be deleted as soon as his name no longer appears in the payroll file.
- Inadequate documentation or labeling may result in the wrong version of a program being modified.

- *Operating System Flaws.*

  Design and implementation errors, system generation and maintenance problems, and deliberate penetrations causing modifications to the operating system can produce undesirable effects in the ERP systems. Flaws in the operating system are often difficult to prevent and detect.

  - User jobs may be permitted to read or write outside the assigned storage area.

- ○ Simultaneous processing of the same file by two jobs may introduce inconsistencies into data.
- ○ An operating system design or implementation error may allow a user to disable audit controls or to access all system information.
- ○ The operating system may not protect a copy of information as thoroughly as it protects the original.
- ○ Unauthorized modification to the operating system may allow a data entry clerk to enter programs and thus subvert the system.
- ○ An operating system crash may expose valuable information such as password lists or authorization tables.
- ○ Maintenance personnel may bypass security controls while performing maintenance work. At such times, the system is vulnerable to errors or intentional acts of the maintenance personnel, or anyone else who might also be on the system and discover the opening (e.g., microcoded sections of the operating system may be tampered with or sensitive information from online files may be disclosed).
- ○ An operating system may fail to record that multiple copies of output have been made from spooled storage devices.
- ○ An operating system may fail to maintain an unbroken audit trail.
- ○ When restarting after a system crash, the operating system may fail to ascertain that all terminal locations are still occupied by the same individuals.
- ○ A user may be able to get into monitor or supervisory mode.
- ○ The operating system may fail to erase all scratch space assigned to a job after the normal or abnormal termination of the job.
- ○ Files may be allowed to be read or written without having been opened.
- *Communications System Failure.*

  Information being routed from one location to another over communication lines is vulnerable to accidental failures and to intentional interception and modification by unauthorized parties.

- *Accidental Failures.*
  - ○ Undetected communication errors may result in incorrect or modified data.
  - ○ Information may be accidentally misdirected to the wrong terminal.
  - ○ Communication nodes may leave unprotected fragments of messages in memory during unanticipated interruptions in processing.
  - ○ Communication protocol may fail to positively identify the transmitter or receiver of a message.
- *Intentional Acts.*
  - ○ Communication lines may be monitored by unauthorized individuals.
  - ○ Data or programs may be stolen via telephone circuits from a remote job entry terminal.
  - ○ Programs in the network switching computers may be modified to compromise security.
  - ○ Data may be deliberately changed by individuals tapping the line (requires some sophistication, but is applicable to financial data).
  - ○ An unauthorized user may take over a computer communication port as an authorized user disconnects from it. Many systems cannot detect the change. This is particularly true in much of the currently available communication equipment and in many communication protocols.
  - ○ If encryption is used, keys may be stolen.
  - ○ A terminal user may be spoofed into providing sensitive data.
  - ○ False messages may be inserted into the system.
  - ○ True messages may be deleted from the system.
  - ○ Messages may be recorded and replayed into the system (i.e., "deposit $100" messages).

Besides the risks described previously, the impact of these additional vulnerabilities must be assessed. These special vulnerabilities pose threats, which are not present at all, or are present to a lesser degree, in non-ERP environments. Once these risks are identified, their severity should be estimated, and controls developed to mitigate their impact on the ERP applications.

INTERNAL CONTROL

Internal control systems are set up to help mitigate against the risks discussed above. The purpose of internal control systems is to reasonably ensure that the following goals are achieved:

- Obligations and costs comply with applicable laws.
- All assets are safeguarded against waste, loss, unauthorized use, and misappropriation.
- Revenues and expenditures that apply to organization operations are recorded and properly accounted for, so that accounts and reliable financial and statistical reports may be prepared and an accounting of these assets may be maintained.

Control Objectives and Key Controls

In order to understand control objectives and key controls, it is important to know what a system of internal controls is. The AICPA Guidelines of Internal Control define it as:

The plan of organization and all the methods and procedures adopted by the management of an entity to assist in achieving management's objective of ensuring, as far as practical, the orderly and efficient conduct of its business, including adherence to management policies, the safeguarding of assets, the prevention and detection of fraud and error, the accuracy and completeness of the accounting records, and the timely preparation of reliable financial information. The system of internal controls extends beyond those matters which relate directly to the functions of accounting system.

Control Objectives

Control objectives are high-level statements of intent by the management to ensure that departmental programs designed to fulfill the organization's strategic plans are carried out effectively and efficiently. These statements of intent embody the plan of organization and all the related systems established by management to safeguard assets, check the accuracy and reliability of financial data, promote operational efficiency and encourage adherence of prescribed management policies.

Once the business risk for the ERP systems is defined, it is possible to determine how these risks will be contained. Control objectives can be defined as "the purpose or justification for having internal controls." The organization's internal control structure must meet several control objectives to prevent, detect and correct errors, omissions and irregularities in business transactions and processes, and to assure continuity of business operations. They are a link between the risks and internal controls.

Control objectives may differ, depending upon the type, scope, and purpose of the audit. There could be several internal control objectives for a given business risk, so that the risk is adequately addressed. Some of the common internal control objectives that an author should look for are:

- Transactions are properly authorized (*Authorized*).
- Transactions are recorded on a timely basis (*Timeliness*).
- Transactions are accurately processed (*Accuracy*).
- All existing transactions are recorded (*Completeness*).
- All recorded transactions are valid (*Validity*).
- Transactions are properly valued (*Valuation*).
- Transactions are properly classified and posted to proper accounts and subsidiary records (*Classification*).
- Transactions are properly summarized and reported (*Reporting*).
- Assets, including software programs, data, human resources, computer facilities, etc. are safeguarded against damage, theft, and so forth (*Security*).
- System and data integrity is maintained (*Integrity*).
- System availability is assured (*Availability*).

- System controllability and auditability is maintained (*Controllability and Auditability*).
- System maintainability is assured (*Maintainability*).
- System usability is assured (*Usability*).
- System economy and efficiency are maintained (*Efficiency*).

Key Controls

Each control objective is met by one or more control techniques. These techniques are the ways and means that management controls the operations, are varied in nature, and exist as:

- *Procedures and policies.*   For example, independent balancing, cancellation of documents after processing, independent signing for approval of prepared source documents, competent and trustworthy personnel, segregation of duties, mandatory vacations, rotation of duty assignments.
- *Information systems design.*   For example, numerically pre-numbered forms, message authentication, console logs, encryption, range and limit checks on input fields.
- *Physical controls.*   For example, combination locks for vaults, card acceptor devices for restricted access areas.
- *Segregation of duties.*

Segregation of Duties

The overall objective of the segregation of duties for ERP systems can be expressed as "production data is only accessible to bonafide users utilizing tested and approved ERP." Bonafide users are those allowed by management to view, update, add or delete transactions in a specific application. The manager in charge of the division or department who relies on the data for its operations owns the data. For instance, the controller owns the financial data; he or she is ultimately responsible for its accuracy and safeguard.

From a practical standpoint, that manager will have devolved the responsibility of granting user access to managers reporting to him or her. These managers will, in turn, rely on a system administrator, either a member of the user department or IT, to brief them on the available functions of the ERP; the identity of the users whose job requires access to these functions; and ultimately, the data. Having understood the sensitivity of the functions and the confidentiality of the data, these managers will delegate authority to the administrator to grant access to users. The IT department is responsible for ensuring that powerful utilities are only accessible to selected users and cannot be utilized in an unauthorized fashion to modify production data. In every environment, there will always be one user and a back-up who have access or can grant themselves access to all data.

These powerful users should be carefully selected and audit trails of their actions should exist. Production data is *never* owned by IT unless it is specific to the operations of the IT department. Production data should only be accessed through authorized utilities that would not allow users to manipulate production data outside of the constraints and controls implemented within the ERP systems. For instance, the rules implemented at the database level require that a customer be in the customer file for their order to be recorded. If a user were able to directly access the order table, through a text editor in a UNIX environment or by TSO/ISPF (True Sharing Option/Interactive System Productivity Facility) in an MVS (Multiple Virtual Storage) environment, the ERP control implemented could be bypassed and an order entered for a nonexistent customer.

Internal Control Summary

Internal controls are methods and procedures adopted by management to achieve its corporate objectives. Thus, the responsibility for ensuring adequate internal controls is part of management's overall responsibility for the day-to-day operations of the organization.

Internal controls techniques can be identified through review of processes, documentation such as policies and procedures, application system's design, and so forth. Obviously, there will be several control techniques identified that will satisfy a given control objective. It is, therefore, important to concentrate only on that technique critical to the satisfaction of the control objective.

Key controls can be defined as "those critical techniques that are acts to compensate, in the eventuality of a failure of every other control technique, for the absence or ineffectiveness of the other control techniques." If these key internal controls are not observed, there is the distinct possibility that the dependent control objective will not be satisfied.

Control objectives are *what* we want to ensure and control techniques are *how* are we going to ensure it.

The minimum level of internal control is divided into the following two levels:

Level 1—General Standards

- *Reasonable assurance.* Internal control systems are to provide reasonable assurance that the objectives of the systems will be accomplished.
- *Supportive attitude.* Managers and employees maintain and demonstrate a positive and supportive attitude toward internal controls at all times.
- *Competent personnel.* Managers and employees have personal and professional integrity and maintain a level of competence that allows them to accomplish their assigned duties, as well as understand the importance of developing and implementing good internal controls.
- *Control objectives.* Internal control objectives are identified or developed for each agency activity and are logical, applicable, and reasonably complete.
- *Control techniques.* Internal control techniques are effective and efficient in accomplishing their internal control objectives.

Level 2—Specific Standards

- *Documentation.* Internal control systems, all transactions and other significant events are clearly documented, and the documentation is readily available for examinations.
- *Recording of transactions and events.* Transactions and other significant events are promptly recorded and properly classified.
- *Execution of transactions and events.* Transactions and other significant events are authorized and executed only by persons acting within the scope of their authority.
- *Separation of duties.* Key duties and responsibilities in authorizing, processing, recording, and reviewing transactions are separated among individuals.

- *Supervision.*   Qualified and continuous supervision is provided to ensure that internal control objectives are achieved.

- *Access to and accountability for resources.*   Access to resources and records is limited to authorized individuals, and accountability for the custody and use of resources is assigned and maintained. Periodic comparison is made between the resources and the recorded accountability to determine whether the two agree. The frequency of the comparison is a function of the vulnerability of the asset.

.

3

ERP Life Cycle

INTRODUCTION

This chapter provides an overview of the generally accepted phases of ERP life cycle (ERPLC). Each phase of this life cycle is defined, including the roles of each principal participant, key activities, and deliverables. Appropriate ERP system control objectives, correlated as criteria in the various phases of the ERPLC, are also presented.

While the concept of an ERPLC is not new, linking it and the generally accepted phase activities to other information processing standards and requirements is not often successfully accomplished. To achieve this objective, IT standards and generally accepted system implementation practices have been structured into an ERPLC model (see Exhibit 3.1 later in this chapter). This model is intended to emphasize control and security activities and deliverables; it is these deliverables or their absence that become the framework of a project review and/or audit.

The ERP life cycle used to implement systems will not be the same in every organization. The operating environment for the ERP life cycle is a function of the organization in which it exists and also varies greatly. Thus, there is no single standard ERPLC methodology. This chapter describes good business practice for the ERPLC and its operating environment. The use of these ERP life cycle concepts and practices should result in a well-controlled and auditable ERP.

ERP AUDITABILITY

Management establishes the environment in which systems are developed, implemented, and operated. If the environment is highly structured, the probability of a well-defined life cycle and compliance with it greatly increases. A loose management style leads to haphazard ERP system practices that may result in serious omissions. The operating environment reflects the adequacy of the general controls over ERP implementation, operations, and maintenance.

Auditability should be a management concern, achieved by proper implementation of management control responsibilities. Auditability relates to the substantial evidential matter produced and retained by an ERP system, as well as the ability to locate and reconstruct processing. Auditability also encompasses the system of internal controls that assures the integrity of processing and the protection of evidential matter.

Auditability takes on greater importance (and difficulty) in ERP because many of these systems have eliminated the traditional source documents. Transactions are originated electronically; auditability depends upon the ability of the system to substantiate the integrity of those input transactions. This integrity is assured only through an adequate system of internal controls.

The concept of auditability requires audit involvement in the implementation of ERP. Retrofitting controls in ERP is expensive and difficult after the fact. Therefore, auditability and effective controls allowing for managerial and audit oversight must be designed and incorporated into ERP as those systems are implemented.

ERPLC METHODOLOGY

The following are generally accepted as the best practices of a good ERPLC methodology:

1. *Predefined documents/deliverables.*

   All of the products or deliverables to be developed during the implementation of an ERP system need to be defined. In the better design methodologies, these products and documents are standardized. They will either be preprinted forms or screens available to the designer on computer terminals. The sequence in which the products are created is also determined. The output of one product or set of products is usually needed before the next product can be developed.

2. *ERP life cycle phases or checkpoints.*

The ERP life cycle should be divided into segments defined by activities, outcomes, or deliverables. Each segment encompasses some part of the development process. The purpose of having distinct phases or checkpoints is to facilitate decisions about completion of the project, changes in direction, cancellation of the project, and authorization for use of more resources on the project at these points in time. This is done to assure that management can continually evaluate project status and make appropriate decisions.

3. *Completion of products/documents are tied to ERP life cycle phase check points.*

Specified work is to be completed at each checkpoint. This work is usually documents to be produced. When a project is reviewed at a checkpoint, it is apparent which products/documents are to be delivered at that point in time. This also helps ensure that the project is on schedule and within budget. The status of work can be determined by examining these checkpoints.

4. *Product document reviews.*

Status reviews of projects are performed by evaluating the deliverables produced by the project team. These products/documents should be produced in a standardized format. These reviews must be signed off upon completion, indicating satisfactory completion of the product/document, and the life cycle phase.

5. *Training is tied to products/documents.*

The training program for people associated with ERP projects is centered on the products/documents to be produced. One needs to understand the ERPLC and its deliverables in order to effectively review the process and outcome. Users and systems maintenance personnel need to understand not only the final system (i.e., its software, hardware, configuration, and controls), but also the requirements definition and analysis process that went into implementing the ERP.

ERPLC CONTROL EVALUATION GUIDE

Before mapping the ERPLC Phases (Project Definition, Requirements Analysis, External Design, Internal Design, Pre-implementation, Implementation, Post-implementation) to the ERPLC Evaluation Control Guide, the structure of the Control Evaluation Guide should be defined. This structure consists of: Business Risks, Control Objectives, Key Controls, Segregation of Duties, and Audit Testing.

Business Risks

A business risk is an exposure that can result in loss due to the occurrence or non-occurrence of an event relating to a business function, activity or transaction. Refer to Chapter 2 for Risk in ERP Systems.

Control Objectives

A control objective for an ERP system is a management goal to ensure that the ERP system is performing its function(s) with appropriate control and security as well as economy, efficiency, and effectiveness.

Once the specific control objectives for an ERP system have been defined, the auditor can use these objectives as criteria against which to review the ERP system implementation. If the control/security goals have been carefully and comprehensively identified, the auditor will have a clear path to follow to determine whether the ERP system, as currently being implemented, will perform satisfactorily or will need significant changes to achieve its control objectives.

Control objectives may differ, depending upon the type, scope, and purpose of the audit. There could be several control objectives for a given business risk so that the risk is adequately addressed. Some of the common control objectives that an author should look for are illustrated below:

- Transactions are properly authorized (*Authorization*).
- Transactions are recorded on a timely basis (*Timeliness*).
- Transactions are accurately processed (*Accuracy*).

- All existing transactions are recorded (*Completeness*).
- All recorded transactions are valid (*Validity*).
- Transactions are properly valued (*Valuation*).
- Transactions are properly classified and posted to proper accounts and subsidiary records (*Classification*).
- Transactions are properly summarized and reported (*Reporting*).
- Assets, including software programs, data, human resources, computer facilities, etc. are safeguarded against damage, theft, and so forth (*Security*).
- System and data integrity is maintained (*Integrity*).
- System availability is assured (*Availability*).
- System controllability and auditability is maintained (*Controllability* and *Auditability*).
- System maintainability is assured (*Maintainability*).
- System usability is assured (*Usability*).
- System economy and efficiency are maintained (*Efficiency*).

Key Controls

A secure ERP system has key controls that:

- Protect its information resources (including hardware, software, firmware, and data) from all significant anticipated threats or hazards.
- Ensure the accuracy and reliability of the data maintained or generated by the ERP system.
- Ensure the operational reliability, as well as accurate and timely performance, of the system.

When they are a data or system concern, controls against threats to confidentiality should be incorporated into the ERP system. The level and type of control/security services sought directly relates to the sensitivity of the information maintained in or produced by the ERP system. The control objectives decided upon correlate strongly with the type of control/security sought for any particular ERP system.

Each control objective is met by one or more control techniques. These techniques are the ways and means that management uses to control the operations; they are varied in nature and exist as:

- *Procedures and policies.*   Independent balancing, cancellation of documents after processing, independent signing for approval of prepared source documents, competent and trustworthy personnel, segregation of duties, mandatory vacations, rotation of duty assignments.
- *Information systems design.*   Numerically pre-numbered forms, message authentication, console logs, encryption, range and limit checks on input fields.
- *Physical controls.*   Combination locks for vaults, card acceptor devices for restricted access areas.
- *Segregation of duties.*

Segregation of Duties

The overall objective of the segregation of duties for ERP systems can be expressed as "production data is only accessible to bonafide users utilizing tested and approved ERP." Bonafide users are those allowed by management to view, update, add, or delete transactions in a specific application. The manager in charge of the division/department who relies on the data for its operations owns the data. For instance, the controller owns the financial data and he or she is ultimately responsible for ensuring its accuracy and security. From a practical standpoint, that manager will have devolved the responsibility of granting user access to managers reporting to him or her. These managers will rely on a system administrator, either a member of the user department or IT, to brief them on the available functions of the ERP, the identity of the users whose job requires access to these functions, and ultimately, the data. Having understood the sensitivity (or lack thereof) of the functions and the confidentiality of the data, these managers will delegate authority to the administrator to grant access to users. The IT department is responsible for ensuring that the powerful utilities are only accessible to selected users and cannot be used in an unauthorized manner to modify production data. In every environment, there will always be one user and a back-up who have access or can grant themselves access, to all data. These powerful users should be carefully selected and audit trails of their actions should exist. Production data is never owned by IT unless it is specific to the operations of the IT department. Production data should only be accessed through authorized utilities that do not allow users to manipulate this data outside of the constraints and controls of the ERP systems. For instance, the ERP program controls implemented at the database level require that a customer be in the customer file for an order to be recorded for the customer. If a user were able to directly access the order table through a text editor, via a UNIX environment or TSO/ISPF in an MVS environment; the control implemented through the ERP could be bypassed and an order entered even for a non-existent customer.

Controls are methods and procedures adopted by the management to achieve its corporate objectives. Thus, the responsibility for ensuring adequate controls is part of management's overall responsibility for the day-to-day operations of the organization.

Control techniques can be identified through the review of processes, documentation such as policies and procedures, the application system's design, and so on. Obviously, there will be several control techniques identified that will satisfy a given control objective. It is, therefore, important to concentrate only on those techniques critical to the satisfaction of the control objective.

Key controls can be defined as "those critical techniques that are enacted to compensate, in the eventuality of a failure of every other control technique, for the absence or ineffectiveness of the other control techniques." If these key controls are not observed, there is the distinct possibility that the dependent control objective will not be satisfied. In summary, control objectives are *what* we want to ensure and control techniques are *how* we are going to ensure it.

Audit Testing

Audit testing is the verification of key control processes to determine whether they are effective in containing risk and providing assurance that the control objective is met.

The objectives of the ERPLC control evaluation are:

- To document risks and control objectives for the total business.
- To relate business risks and control objectives to key controls for the particular ERP system/procedure.
- To document key controls for the particular ERP application.
- To relate key controls to audit tests.

BENEFITS OF CONTROL EVALUATION GUIDE DEVELOPMENT FOR ERP APPLICATIONS

Benefits include:

- Shared and complete understanding of the high-level business risks and control objectives that pertain to the auditable entity.
- Overall, coordinated identification of key controls, both manual and automated, in support of specific lines of business.
- Stabilization of terms and definitions.
- Uniform communication among various participants.
- Shared responsibility in the CEG development process among various participants.
- Feedback mechanism for ERP System auditing with respect to quality and value of the CEG delivered to its specific clients.
- Overall, coordinated identification of control weaknesses during ERP system review that is communicated to the project team for attention.

Now that there is a structure for the Control Evaluation Guide, ERP life cycle can be reviewed. Without structure, the deliverables to be produced and their timeframe cannot be determined. Structure also ensures that necessary requirements are identified and controls installed. Exhibit 3.1a–b provides the overview of the ERPLC and is designed to be used in the following manner:

- As a tool for understanding: It defines the major phases in the ERP life cycle in terms of key activities to be performed and products delivered. This exhibit can be used to orient the auditor to the ERPLC process by explaining the:
  - Phases/activities of the ERPLC process.
  - Participants (i.e., functional responsibilities for implementation rather than job titles or full-time positions) in the ERPLC process.
  - Responsibilities assigned to individual participants.
  - Products/deliverables to be produced.
- As a framework for structuring and understanding the proposed review methodology.

Exhibit 3.1a   ERP Project Life Cycle (Audit View)

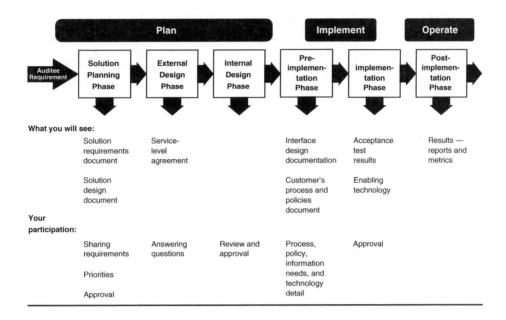

- As a framework for customizing an audit methodology to a specific ERP.
- As the criteria for evaluating ERP under implementation and post-implementation.

As a basis for structuring this control evaluation guide, refer to Exhibits 3.2. and 3.3. These exhibits can be used by audit to understand how to review the ERP implementation. Actual reviews, however, must be tied to the particular ERP implementation methodology used by the organization for the ERP system under review. This is because audit cannot expect that ERP systems will be implemented in accordance with any specific ERPLC methodology.

Audits of ERP system life cycle are not practical unless well-defined documentation exists. ERP system documentation requirements are a classic problem associated with the implementation of any ERP system. It is critical that the purpose and functions of the documents elaborated on below are achieved.

The six ERP life cycle phases shown in exhibit 3.2 are intended to clarify the broad functions or activities that should occur during the

Exhibit 3.1b   ERP Project Life Cycle (Implementation View)

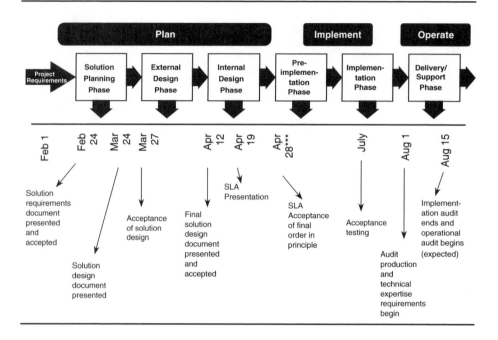

implementation of an ERP system. They cover activities commonly performed, so that whatever implementation methodology audit encounters, the ERPLC encompasses the activities likely to be found. It could, thus, be customized to a specific audit.

The material above lays the groundwork for the rest of this chapter. It does this by presenting the unique risks in an ERP environment, a detailed description of the phase activities in a generally accepted ERPLC for an ERP implementation, and the need for and sources of control objectives for a well-controlled ERP during implementation. The remainder of this chapter gives the auditor detailed guidance on performing a responsible and successful ERPLC audit.

The ERPLC methodology described here is conceptual. It incorporates good practices from many different methodologies into one approach. From an audit perspective, it defines the type of documentation needed to ensure auditability, and the presence of other requisite controls of an ERP system.

Audit involved in ERP implementation reviews should not expect to find the ERP implementation precisely according to the methodology

Exhibit 3.2a

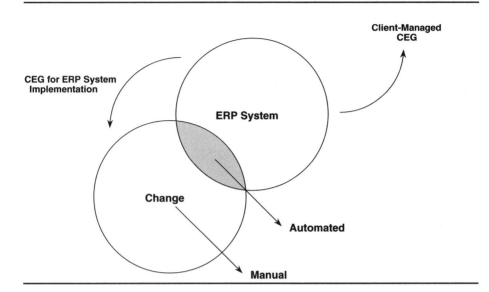

described here. It should, however, expect that the methodology used by its organization or the organization under review, encompasses the best parts/documents of the methodology described. If the ERPLC methodology is deficient, audit should recommend improvements.

Audit has two tasks to perform In reviewing the ERPLC methodology used to implement the ERP system, audit has two tasks to perform:

1. Audit must make a preliminary review of the ERPLC for its adequacy in providing the discipline and control over the ERP implementation as described here.

2. Audit must compare the ERPLC being used for the ERP under review with this methodology for coverage of its provisions and adequacy of the ERP controls.

Audit, as the representative of management, must convert each of management's control objectives into appropriate audit questions that will enable a determination of whether the particular area of control has been achieved. For example, in Phase I, Project Definition and Requirements Analysis, a project plan must be created that is adequate

Exhibit 3.2a   Mapping of the ERP Project to the ERPLC Audit Phase for CEG Development

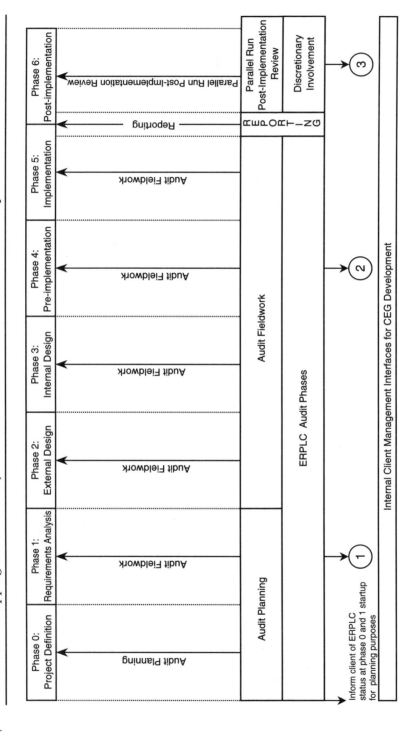

Exhibit 3.2b CEG Development: Identification of Business Risks and Control Objectives

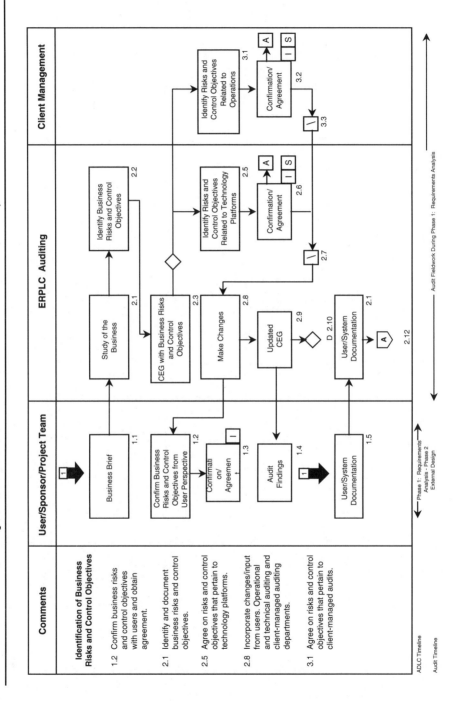

57

Exhibit 3.2c CEG Development: Identification of Key Controls

58

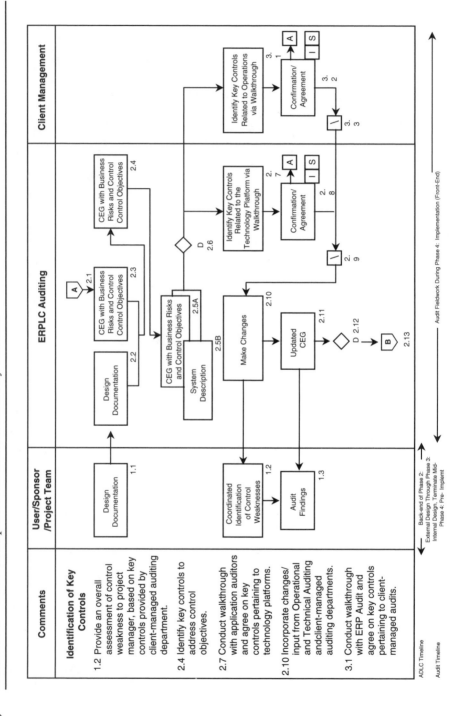

Exhibit 3.2d CEG Development: Identification of Audit Tests

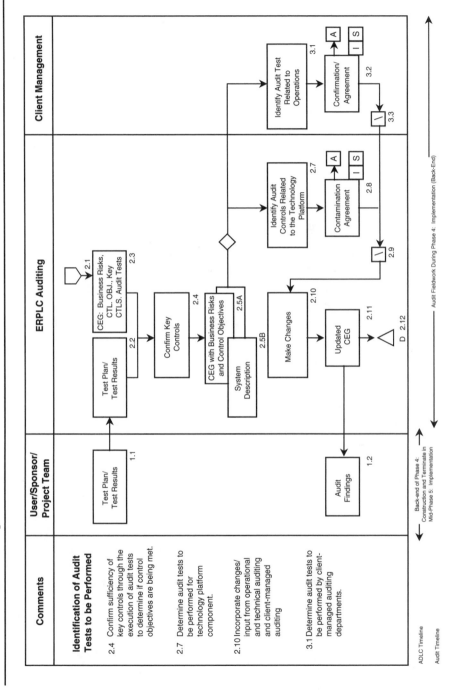

for maintaining control over the project throughout its implementation and operational life (i.e., its ERPLC). In order to assure that this goal is achieved, audit must ascertain that such a project plan has been created, that it includes a comprehensive work schedule of project activities; that appropriate acceptance test points throughout the ERPLC have been identified; that the evaluation and approval procedures have been defined at each of these points; and that the project plan is in compliance with the organization's ERPLC methodology. Audit Test Tables in Appendixes 3A, 3B, and 3C are translations of control objectives into suitable audit questions.

PHASE I—PROJECT DEFINITION AND REQUIREMENTS ANALYSIS

In real life situations, a project is rarely well defined and is not normally delineated in distinct phases as prescribed in the ERPLC. What is usually the case is that the project sponsor will assign the project responsibilities to a project manager who will then identify activities and deliverables. Each deliverable will be the building block of the entire project.

The challenge to the auditor is to delineate these activities into auditable units which then becomes the basis for each of the phases prescribed in the ERPLC. Exhibit 3.3 presents the project definition and requirements analysis.

Hidden Costs

In practice, ERP systems can be difficult to deploy and maintain. ERP packages are complex by nature and IT departments must invariably tailor the software to fit the company's specific requirements and business processes. Installing an ERP system is usually a massive undertaking measured not in months, but in years. Even after the initial deployment, an ERP system must be continually adapted to reflect changes in the business and software upgrades and extensions.

Due to their complexity, ERP projects are expensive. Before embarking on an ERP project, it is important to understand the project's total cost of ownership (TCO), which extends far beyond the price of the ERP software. In a survey of 63 companies, it was found that the average TCO was $15 million for ERP when real project costs such as software, staff time, consulting, and hardware were included.

Exhibit 3.3   Phase I — Project Definition and Requirements Analysis

Risk	Business Impact	Expected Controls

1. The scope of the project is not adequately defined.
2. Cost/benefit analysis has not been completed.
3. The implementation strategy (e.g., customization) has not been adequately analyzed for a new system.
4. The ERPLC and project management processes have not been adequately defined.
5. Project risk factors have not been identified and addressed.
6. Project costs, resources and key milestones have not been estimated.
7. A detailed project plan has not been developed for the ERPLC phase.
8. Vendors' performance expectations have not been defined and/or a monitoring process established (if applicable).
9. Business requirements have not been clearly defined.
10. Control and operational requirements have not been considered.
  • Changes to critical standing data are not fully authorized, identified, and reviewed by an independent person
  • Authorization limits are not built in or monitored
	1. The system is not delivered on time, within budget (including additional vendor costs), and/or with the desired functionality, as well as poor quality system components are delivered.
	2. Development resources are invested in a project with a lower business justification than other projects.
		1. A Statement of Work Document is completed which describes:
		  • Description and scope of project
		  • Cost/benefit analysis and business ss justification for project
		  • Development strategy for new systems.
		  • ERPLC methodology to be followed
		  • Project management process, including the assignment of a project manager and team, including (1) users—Accounting, Compliance, etc., if they are impacted (2) ERP systems team personnel, (3) Security Officer and Program Office personnel, maintenance of project plans, issues tracking, change requests and periodic status reporting. As part of this, consultants and vendors should be managed.
		  • Project risk factors and steps to address them
		  • Estimated project milestones, resources requirements (e.g., staffing), and costs
		2. A detailed project plan has been developed including all the tasks/deliverables discussed below as well as vendor related tasks.
		3. There is a defined process for implementation the RFP and vendor selection.

(continued)

Exhibit 3.3   Phase I — Project Definition and Requirements Analysis (*Continued*)

Risk	Business Impact	Expected Controls
• No automated confirmation of address changes • Sensitive override transactions are not supported, identified and reviewed by an independent person • The quality review of sensitive information is not risk based or the sample size is too small to be effective • Critical data fields are not edited for accuracy and completeness • Edits in front-end and back-end systems are not consistent. 11. A conversion strategy has not been developed (if applicable). 12. User and system management have not approved the business requirements. 13. Project plans have not been developed. 14. An end stage review was not performed to access the status of the project and identify any action plans required.	3. The system is not delivered on time, within budget and/or with the desired functionality, as well as poor quality system components delivered. 4. Application and operational controls are not adequate.	4. A vendor contract has been reviewed by Legal Department, which addresses the following: • Roles and responsibilities • Vendor's system access requirements • Compliance with technology standards (e.g., security) • Ownership of programs as well as escrow agreements if the codes is not owned. • If a service bureau, right of auditability, including receiving SAS 70 reports. • Service level expectations, including timeliness, quality and the process for requesting changes. • Problem resolution procedures • Confidentiality agreement 5. A process is in place to review and track vendor bills and performance. 6. Detailed business requirements have been documented that include: • Application/operational control impact analysis and requirements, including controls over key/sensitive transactions, application security, and reconciliations. • Manual workarounds should not be part of business requirements unless approved by senior management

- Changes to critical standing data are fully authorized, identified, and reviewed by an independent person
- Authorization limits are built in and monitored
- Automated confirmation of address changes
- Sensitive override transactions are supported, identified and reviewed by an independent person
- Quality review of sensitive information is risk based or the sample size is large enough to be effective
- Critical data fields are edited for accuracy and completeness
- Edits in font-end and back-end systems are consistent
- System operational requirements including IT, disaster recovery/BCP and performance requirements. Representatives from Information Security and Business Continuation Planning should be involved with assessing these requirements.

7. User communities have actively participated in the development of the business requirements. Both user and system management have formally approved (e.g., sign-off) the business requirements.

(continued)

Exhibit 3.3   Phase I — Project Definition and Requirements Analysis (*Continued*)

Risk	Business Impact	Expected Controls
		8. Both user and system management have formally approved (e.g., sign-off) the business requirements. As part of this, there should be a walkthrough performed by systems and users to ensure they fully understand the requirements being requested. 9. A conversion strategy has been documented including: • Review and clean-up of existing data • Automated/manual conversion requirements • Quality review/reconciliation requirements 10. A detailed project plan has been developed (including all the tasks/deliverbles discussed below). 11. An end stage review should be performed: • To ensure that the project is on schedule/budget and if not, develop appropriate action plans • Review the impact of change requests on the project • Review and develop action plans for outstanding project issues

In order to avoid out-of-control costs and incomplete results, management must understand an ERP system's hidden costs and the major issues involved with implementing a project. The following are several key areas where problems can arise:

Understanding of the Problem

- The decision to pursue a solution is based upon a clear understanding of the problem and a comparison of expected benefits versus costs of the solution.
- A needs statement describes, in written form, deficiencies in existing capabilities, new or changed program requirements, or opportunities for increased economy and efficiency.

Note: While the focus of the Project Plan is on the implementation of the ERP system, the plan must consider the ERP system's installation and operation, especially the certification process the ERP system must go through prior to placement into the production environment (i.e., going operational). A formal certification plan should be included as a routine subsection of the project plan for all subsystems/modules designated as sensitive. That subsection contains clarification of responsibilities, security requirements, and evaluation and testing approach, schedule and support required, as well as identification of the evaluation products. Just as the remainder of the project plan is to be reviewed and modified during each phase, so the certification plan is to be revised as needed, based on the updated risk analysis.

The Project Plan

- Specifies the strategy for managing the ERP Implementation.
- Defines the goals and activities for all phases and sub-phases.
- Includes resource estimates over the duration of ERP implementation, and intermediate milestones including management and technical reviews (i.e., for security, privacy, and internal control requirements).

- Defines methods for design, documentation, problem reporting, and change control.
- Specifies supporting techniques and tools.
- Describes the unique ERPLC methodology to be used during the life of the particular project.

The Risk Analysis

- Evaluates the risk analysis as well as the risk or sensitivity of the data/information in, or resources controlled by, the proposed ERP system.
- Identifies control and specific security requirements based on the ERP system's sensitivity or criticality.
- Identifies control and security vulnerabilities of an ERP system, determines the nature and magnitude of associated threats to data and assets, determines the resulting potential for loss, and provides project managers, system security specialists, and auditors with recommended countermeasures.

Audit Concerns

The risk analysis is commonly modified in later phases. Audit should be vigilant about risk analysis areas, and specific tests need to be performed to validate the risks exposed; these are commonly modified in later phases as a better understanding of the problem is gained. The risk analysis should be reviewed and updated, as necessary, during each phase of the ERPLC to assure that no new vulnerabilities have emerged and that appropriate security measures have been installed. During the ERP security and certification reviews, audit should use the findings and recommendations of the risk analysis. This should be prepared and maintained as a separate document, and reviewed and updated as necessary when the operational ERP system or operating environment is modified.

The audit plan:

- Encompasses all system activities within the organization.
- Clarifies audit involvement that may range from review of completed work products at each phase to active review participation in each phase.

- Emphasizes the overall objective to assess the adequacy of the control framework and provide reasonable assurances to management of the effectiveness, integrity, and security of the ERP system implementation.

Legal Requirements

It is important to provide reasonable assurance that the ERP system will conform to legal requirements. Legal requirements applicable to the ERP system may originate from various sources such as local and national privacy statutes, which may restrict collection and use of certain types of information about individuals. Safeguards are obviously necessary in such systems. Conversely, organizations subject to statutes that provide for responses to legitimate requests for information, should have systems designed for timely responses. In the United States, the Freedom of Information Act is such a statute. The applicability of any national standards program to the ERP system ishould also be considered by audit. The United States has a Federal Information Processing Standards (FIPS) program that must be observed by federal ERP systems. If such standards apply, they should be included in the audit review to assure management that these requirements have been considered and satisfied.

Management Policies

It is necessary to provide reasonable assurance that the ERP system can carry out the policies prescribed by management. Management should establish policies on what is expected of ERP systems and audit should determine whether they are being followed. Audit should also review the provisions for security required by management to protect data and programs against unauthorized access and modification.

If management's requirements are not being met, or have not been clearly articulated; audit must report shortcomings so that corrective actions can be taken.

Control Framework

The control framework provides reasonable assurance that the ERP system includes controls necessary to protect against loss or serious error and add to the efficiency and economy of the operation. The auditor's review should also focus on whether the ERP system will produce desired results at minimum cost. This includes reviewing:

- Statement of mission needs and system objectives.
- Feasibility study and evaluation of alternatives to meet needs and objectives.
- Cost/benefit analysis that attributes specific benefits and costs to alternatives.

Audit Trails

It is important to provide reasonable assurance that the ERP system provides the controls and audit trails needed for management, operational, and audit reviews. In financial systems, a transaction must be capable of being traced from its initiation, through all intermediate processing steps, to the resulting financial statements. Similarly, information in the financial statements must be traceable to its origin. Such capability is referred to by various terms (e.g., audit trail, management trail, and transaction trail) and is also essential in nonfinancial systems. The reliability of the output can be properly assessed when the transaction processing flow can be traced and the controls over it, both manual and ERP-oriented, can be evaluated.

Documentation

ERP systems take a long time to deploy and are used for many years within a company. They usually outlast the IT employees and business-process managers who conceptualize, deploy, and modify the systems. Documenting the system is crucial so that future employees can make sense of the software and business-process logic the system encompasses. Documentation is also needed to help future workers deal with the inevitable updates, extensions, and integration projects that occur as a company evolves. In addition, documentation can save consultant's time and help them map the scope of projects properly to improve cost accountability.

It is important to provide reasonable assurance that the ERP system is documented in a manner that permits appropriate maintenance and audit reviews.

ERP system procedures should produce documentation sufficient to define:

- Programs that will do processing in the system.
- Data files to be processed.
- Reports to be prepared.
- Instructions to be used by computer operators.
- Instructions to user groups for preparation and control of data.

> **Note:** Management policy provides for evaluation of documentation and the adequacy of testing before it is made operational.

Project Management

Project management includes:

- Planning and controlling system or process development.
- Monitoring and directing the project during implementation. Project management should ensure that the needs of the user are met by the project, and that all relevant issues are brought to the attention of management.

It is a high-level concern that a means for monitoring and directing the project during development and implementation is established and followed.

Planning and Project Management

It takes time and effort to properly prepare for an ERP deployment. The company's IT staff and the appropriate business managers must be given the time and clear responsibility to conceive and evaluate the project's scope, costs, and timeline. It is important to assign the planning responsibilities to staff members who not only have a good grasp of the technology, but also understand the company's business requirements and processes. Whoever leads the planning should see the project through, from the initial deployment to some extended period after deployment to work out the inevitable kinks.

Integration

The concept of integration lies at the very heart of ERP. The original idea was to create an application that combined an integrated database, code set, and user interface to tie together essential corporate information and business processes. It makes sense that integration would also be extended to include software from other enterprise providers. Integrating two applications from the same vendor is a challenge; integrating applications from a variety of vendors is even more difficult.

To reduce the difficulty of connecting their systems with other vendors' applications, organizations have urged their primary ERP providers to adopt a more open and flexible architecture and to support standards-based computing. Most big ERP providers have responded by migrating their architectures to component frameworks based on standards such as COM and CORBA. COM is Component Object Model, Microsoft's strategic building block for developing application programs. CORBA is Common Object Request Broker Architecture, an architecture and specification for creating, distributing, and managing distributed program objects in a network. COM and CORBA are explained further at the end of this chapter. However, in the vast majority of cases, it is still quite difficult, expensive, and time-consuming to integrate enterprise software.

When it comes to opening their architectures, vendors are of two minds. On the one hand, they need to respond to customer demands for easier integration. By supporting integration with other vendors' software, they can add diverse functions to the customers' ERP systems without having to develop every new application. On the other hand, it is easier for vendors to provide efficient and reliable software when they control all the pieces. ERP vendors also make more money when they sell more modules to individual customers. While the trend is definitely toward increasing openness, it will not happen overnight. Vendors cannot abruptly migrate to a new architecture because that would disenfranchise customers with legacy systems.

Traditionally, only managers responsible for specific functions—finance, human resources, manufacturing, and so forth—had access to a company's ERP systems. But that is starting to change as companies recognize that sharing the information in their ERP systems can reduce costs, increase efficiency, and improve relationships with their various stakeholders. As a result, ERP is now opening up to users in other companies, self-service users, and mobile users. Expanding access to new groups of users inevitably means changes to business process that should be evaluated before adding these capabilities. For example, if your company is not prepared to share data with suppliers and other business partners, these capabilities are pointless.

Before making a decision on ERP packages, make a list of software needed to integrate and the specific functions, business process, and data that need to be tied together. Carefully determine how much work is involved to integrate those packages and get a clear understanding of the vendor's timetable for supporting the integration of any problematic functions.

Companies almost always underestimate the time and cost necessary for enterprise software integration. ERP systems rarely exist in a vacuum; they usually need to be tied into software and complex business processes that predate the ERP system. In addition to software from a primary ERP vendor, the enterprise may also want to use applications provided by other software vendors. For example, a company may want to tie its core ERP suite from SAP into a customer relationship management (CRM) application. Mergers and acquisitions also create difficult integration challenges because the merged companies may use different ERP packages and applications with which they have already integrated. A large enterprise typically operates five or more ERP systems and some companies have more than 20 ERP systems.

Managing Consultants

Since few IT departments are staffed to handle the extra work required to implement each phase of a big ERP project, many of the items mentioned earlier require consultants. Without proper management, consulting fees can eat through your budget faster than a pack of mice through a chunk of cheese. It is important to make sure that in-house staff is capable of managing consultants.

Consulting contracts should carefully define:

- Key deliverables and schedules.
- Skill levels of available staff.
- Objectives for training internal staff.

The contract should also contain a detailed specification that clearly points out the desired business objective and technical requirements. Proper planning and project management are important for managing consultants and holding them accountable.

PHASE II—EXTERNAL DESIGN

Phase II of the ERPLC is the external design phase, as shown in Exhibit 3.4.

Specification of the Problem

- Provides a specific high-level definition including information aggregates, information flows, and logical processing steps, as well as all major interfaces, their inputs and outputs.

Functional Requirements

- Provides a basis for mutual understanding between users and implementers of the initial definition of the ERP system, including the requirements, operating environment, and the implementation plan.
- Includes the proposed methods and procedures, a summary of improvements, a summary of impacts, security, privacy, and internal control considerations, cost considerations, and alternatives.
- Includes the functions required of the software in quantitative terms and how these functions satisfy the performance objectives.
- Specifies the performance requirements vis-à-vis accuracy, validation, timing, and flexibility. Explains inputs/outputs, as well as data characteristics.

The Risk Analysis

The risk analysis should be reviewed and updated, as necessary, during each phase of the ERPLC to assure that no new vulnerabilities have emerged and that appropriate security measures have been installed. It should be prepared and maintained as a separate document. Reviews should be scheduled when modification is made to the operational ERP system or operating environment. Audit, during the ERP security and certification reviews, should use the findings and recommendations of the risk analysis.

PHASE III—INTERNAL DESIGN

Phase III is the internal design phase, which includes:

- Building and creating the development, test and production environments with respective change management controls in place.
- Process re-engineering, which involves incorporating the detailed design specifications into the ERP systems and fine-tuning ERP software.

The ERP system internal design includes the following steps:

1. Defining the processing to be done by the ERP.
2. Designing the processing steps.
3. Determining the data input and files that will be required.
4. Specifying each individual ERP's module input data and output.
5. Specifying the approach to and details of the implementation of the ERP system including business processes re-engineering to fit the ERP systems.

Each area must be properly controlled, consistent with good management practices (see Exhibit 3.4).

Specifications for Internal Control and Security

The following three points need to be addressed when creating specifications:

1. Specifications for the control framework and security requirements define the security and internal control needs of the system, based both on vulnerabilities identified during the risk analysis and established security and internal control standards.
2. All security and internal controls, including general controls (i.e., management and environmental controls)

Exhibit 3.4 Exhibit Phase — Design Phase

Risk	Business Impact	Expected Controls
1. Compliance with enterprise IT standards were not considered.	1. The system is not delivered on time, within budget, and/or with the desired functionality, as well as poor quality system components delivered functionality.	1. The hardware, software and development tools used are compliant with enterprise standards, or the appropriate deviation request was filed and approved.
2. Future production support requirements (e.g., programmer access to production) was not considered.	2. Application and operational controls are not adequate.	2. An analysis was performed to ensure that the system software components, database, and application meet the enterprise Information Security standards. Representatives from Information Security should be included in this assessment.
3. Application/operational control requirements were not considered in the design.	3. Inadequate documentation exists to develop and maintain the system in the future.	3. A Library Management process was defined which is compliant with the Enterprise standard, including the use of an approved tool, limited programmer access to the test environment and version control. Representatives from the Library Program Office should be included in the development of the process. Specifically, select, key Enterprise-wide Program Change Control and Library Management Process controls consist of the following:
4. System documentation was not created or is inadequate.		
5. Automated and manual procedures to support conversion requirements have not been adequately developed.		• A completed, approved change request form (paper or electronic) is maintained before ERP Implementation begins. This Change Request Form is used to track the status of change requests, and this tracking is part of the Change Management function.
6. Comprehensive test plans have not been developed.		
7. Detailed project plans have not been developed for the Testing Phase.		
8. An end stage review was not performed to assess the status of the project and identify any action plans required.		• Access to test, production, and operating programs and files is restricted to only those users who require such access, based on current responsibilities.

Risk	Business Impact	Expected Controls
		• Version control is enforced throughout the ERP system life cycle and production environment.
		• Only approved software versions are moved into production.
		• The Release Manager role and Library Management Administration role cannot modify application controls.
		• Developers are not permitted production access or installation rights for security and control purposes.
		• All changes and approvals are documented detailing the changes made, indicating name of individual and date of change.
		• An emergency fix must be a documented, controlled process.
		• Individuals cannot approve their own work.
		• An individual is allowed to approve the promotion of code only once during the ERP life cycle. (However, when an individual. Fulfills the Project Manager role exclusively, he may potentially approve the promotion of code more than once.)
		4. Interface comply with enterprise standards for header and trailer records as well as monitoring of file transmission (including automated rejection of incomplete files).
		5. Sensitive interface files transmitted over public networks are encrypted.
		6. Production Support requirements (including hardware, back-up, performance, etc.) have been defined and have been discussed with Relationship Managers. In

(continued)

Exhibit 3.4 Exhibit Phase — Design Phase (*Continued*)

Risk	Business Impact	Expected Controls
		addition, the application design will not require programmers to perform production support functions. 7. Application/operational control requirements were included in the application design, including controls over key/sensitive transactions, application security and reconciliations. 8. The following system documentation required by enterprise standards was created: • screen and report design specifications • data retention requirements • technical architecture definition • system and program flowcharts • program/module specifications • file/database definitions 9. A conversion plan has been developed, including defining automated and manual conversion tasks, error handling/correction procedures, as well as quality review and reconciliation tasks. 10. A detailed test plan has been developed which includes the following: • coverage of all key functionality defined in the business requirements • negative testing (e.g., invalid data transactions) • period processing (e.g., month end, year end) • regression testing (for major enhancements to existing systems) • system interfaces

Risk	Business Impact	Expected Controls
		• application and operational controls
		• manual workarounds for missing functionality
		• automated and manual conversion procedures
		• performance requirements, including volume and stress testing
		• operational requirements, such as the batch cycle
		• back-up and recovery
		• Testing integration test lab if software will be rolled out to different client configurations
		11. The test plan has been reviewed and approved by users and systems management prior to the start of testing.
		12. A detailed project plan has been developed for the Construction and Testing phase (including all the tasks/deliverables discussed below).
		13. An end stage review should be performed:
		• to ensure that the project is on schedule/budget, and if not, develop appropriate action plans
		• review the impact of change requests on the project
		• review and develop action plans for outstanding project issues

need to be defined and approved prior to starting formal construction and implementation of the ERP system.

3. Security specifications should be reviewed and approved by all parties involved in the use or operation of the ERP System.

Specifications for the Data Requirements

Two main points need to be addressed when creating specifications for data requirements:

1. *Define data descriptions and technical information about data collection requirements.* The data description is normally separated into two categories: static and dynamic data. Data elements in each category are normally arranged in logical groupings, such as functions, subjects, or other groupings most relevant to their use. The data description also describes the type of information required to document the characteristics of each data element, and specifies information to be collected by the user and that to be processed by the ERP system.

2. *Address procedures for data collection and the impacts of the data requirements are addressed.* The importance of data sensitivity/criticality assessments is a prelude to postulating the nature and magnitudes of threats and the analysis of the costs to contain them.

The Risk Analysis

The risk analysis should be reviewed and updated, as necessary, during each phase of the ERPLC to assure that no new vulnerabilities have emerged and that appropriate security measures have been installed. Audit, during the ERP security and certification reviews should use the findings and recommendations of the risk analysis. It should be prepared and maintained as a separate document, and should be reviewed and updated as necessary, when modification is made to the operational ERP system or operating environment.

> **Note:**   All specifications should be precise so that tests can be designed to verify that the requirements were satisfied.

PHASE IV—PRE-IMPLEMENTATION

Phase IV is the pre-implementation phase, as shown in Exhibit 3.5.

Testing

Given the critical nature of a company's ERP system, it should be thoroughly tested before it is fully deployed. Do not just test the system with dummy data. Use actual data from different real-world scenarios. For example, a manufacturing company should pull up historic orders from customers and route the orders through the entire process of creating the product, shipping it, and billing for it. Ideally, employees who actually operate the specific business processes on a day-to-day basis should perform these tests. Of course, all of this costs money, but the investment will significantly reduce other costs that result from downtime and poor implementations that occur when systems are not properly tested.

Dirty Data

A number of problems and hidden costs crop up when handling real-world data. When an enterprise converts its legacy systems to ERP, it must convert large amounts of data for use in the new system. Much of the old data is difficult, if not impossible, to convert, which means a lot of time and money will be spent re-entering it into the system or putting it through complex conversion processes. Even after a system is fully deployed, you cannot take the data for granted because it ages. For instance, every month some of the company's customers, employees, and business partners change their address or other parts of their profile. The rule of thumb is that about 2 percent of a company's customer data goes bad every month. Therefore, an ongoing effort is required to clean up obsolete data. When data is combined from multiple systems for analysis or as a result of integration projects, more work can be involved to clean it up and convert it.

Test plans for the testing of the ERP system include detailed specifications, descriptions, and procedures for all tests, as well as test data reduction, and criteria for the evaluation of the quality and correctness of the ERP system, as shown in Exhibit 3.6.

Integration and system testing of the ERP System occurs and the system is executed on a test data.

Exhibit 3.5   Phase IV — Pre-implementation Review

Risk	Business Impact	Expected Controls
1. Inadequate and/or incomplete testing was performed.	1. The ERP system does not function as intended.	1. Adequate resources have been assigned to execute the test plan, including specific test responsibilities assigned to individuals.
2. Test results were not reviewed and/or approved by user and systems management.	2. Incomplete and/or inaccurate data is converted.	2. A process is in place to monitor the execution of the test plan (e.g., all components were executed), as well as to track, prioritize and correct errors. Note: All high risk errors must be corrected and tested, or manual workarounds developed and tested, prior to the system being moved into production.
3. A review and clean-up of existing data was not performed.	3. Conversion procedures do not function as intended.	
4. A mock conversion was not performed.	4. Version control of programs moved into the test environment are inadequate and/or the potential for unauthorized program changes being made exists.	
5. Enterprise library management standards were not complied with.		3. A review and clean-up of existing data was performed.
6. An end stage review was not performed to assess the status of the project and identify any action plans required.	5. Inaccurate and/or incomplete data conversion.	4. A mock conversion was performed, including quality review and reconciliation tasks.
7. A detailed project plan has not been developed for the implementation phase.	6. Ineffective control procedures are implemented.	5. The library management process defined during the Design phase, is being adhered to.
8. Data conversion was not successfully completed.	7. The system is not ready for production implementation.	
9. ERP System requirements, including a runbook, have not been adequately addressed.	8. Inability to recover from processing problems.	6. User and system management have reviewed and formally approved (e.g , sign-off) the test results.
10. IT disaster recovery and business continuity plans have not been updated.		7. A training plan for users and systems personnel has been developed.
11. User procedures have not been updated or developed.		8. A detailed project plan has been developed for the Implementation phase (including all the tasks and deliverables discussed below).
12. Application security has not been assigned/restricted based on job responsibilities.		9. An end stage review should be performed:
13. System level security controls are not adequate.		• To ensure that the project is on schedule/budget and if not, develop appropriate action plans
		• Review the impact of change requests on the project
		• Review and develop action plans for outstanding project issues.

Risk	Business Impact	Expected Controls

14. System and user management did not formally approve the system for production implementation.
15. A fallback plan does not exist in the event of processing problems.
		10. A process is in place to monitor the execution of the conversion plan, including quality review and reconciliation tasks, as well as to track, prioritize and correct errors. Note: All high risk errors must be corrected and tested prior to the system being moved into production.
		11. A runbook should be developed which describes the following:
		  • Interface files sent/received, and related control procedures to ensure that files were sent/received and that the input files are complete.
		  • Batch process, including the use of an automated job scheduler, and monitoring procedures to ensure all jobs were executed.
		  • Service level agreements and performance monitoring
		  • Problem management, including the formal tracking of problems
		  • An emergency contact list and access procedure, including post management review and password resets.
		  • Release management (e.g., production implementation of program changes)
		  • Back-up and recovery, including the frequency, tracking, and off-site storage of back-ups.
		12. The IT disaster recovery plan is updated, including:
		  • Ensuring that adequate back-up servers are stored in an alternate processing location

(continued)

Exhibit 3.5   Phase IV — Pre-implementation Review (*Continued*)

Risk	Business Impact	Expected Controls
		• Interface files can be rerouted to the alternate processing site.
		• Copy the IT disaster recovery plan and the runbook are stored at the alternate processing location.
		13. The business continuity plan is updated, including:
		• Recovery time objectives
		• The adequacy of the alternate processing facilities (e.g., can it support the needed number of people)
		• Impact on computer related processing, such as new hardware/software requirements (e.g. workstations).
		• Copy of the business continuity plan is stored at the alternate processing location.
		14. User operational and control procedures have been updated to reflect the controls key controls built into the system as well as manual workarounds (identified during business requirements and design).
		15. Security, change control, and business continuity planning have been addressed for any manual workarounds.
		16. Application owners have been identified and have reviewed and approved the security profiles established.
		17. Application owners have been identified and have reviewed and approved the security profiles established.
		18. Individuals have been assigned access based on their job function and related security profile.

Risk	Business Impact	Expected Controls
		19. An application security administrator and back-up have been assigned to grant terminations) application access.
		20. Application security administration procedures have been developed including granting and maintaining (e.g., transfers and terminations) application access.
		21. Standard access request forms/templates have been updated to reflect the new security profiles.
		22. System-level security control features (e.g., Windows NT, Win2000 and UNIX) are effectively utilized for critical application and database services (See UNIX and Windows NT, Win2000 best practices for specific controls).
		23. System-level access to production programs, data (files and database) and the job scheduler have been adequately restricted.
		24. System and user management have formally approved the production implementation of the system.
		25. A fallback plan exists which describes how to fallback to the previous version/application as well as reprocess transactions.
		26. A list is maintained of system fixes and enhancements that need to be performed in the future.
		27. The application has been added, with sufficient details, to databases.
		28. A final review was performed to ensure that expected benefits were achieved and budgeted costs were met.

Exhibit 3.6   Testing Application Controls

CONTROLS OVER SYSTEM STANDING DATA (E.G., TABLE UPDATES)
- Limited update capability
- Authorized supporting documentation for changes
- System generated report/audit trail of changes
- Independent review of changes made against authorizing documentation

CONFIRMATIONS
- Confirmations are generated for all financial transactions and address changes
- Confirmations cannot be suppressed

EDITS OF KEY FIELDS
- Key data fields (e.g., social security number, date of birth, etc.) should be required and validated for reasonableness. Key data fields would have a regulator or processing impact if they were not present or were incorrect.
- Duplicate transactions should be identified and, where possible, rejected (there maybe legitimate duplicates)
- Edits should reject data rather than give informational warnings.

QUALITY REVIEW/CONTROLS
- Sensitive transactions (e.g., financial, regulatory) are reviewed on a sample basis for accuracy, completeness, and authorization
- Results of these reviews are reported and analyzed to identify root case. Appropriate action plans are developed.

OVERRIDES
- Instances in which overrides are acceptable are defined and documented
- If there is a regulator impact (e.g., prospectus requirements) the acceptable instances for overrides are reviewed by Legal
- Access to override functions is limited to management/supervisory personnel

RECONCILIATIONS
- Reconciliations are performed for financial transactions transmitted between systems

PAYMENT LIMITS
- Payment limits are enforced by the system (e.g., claims processor is limited to $99,999.00)
- The amounts of the limits should be based on experience and level of responsibility

---

(continued)

Exhibit 3.6   Testing Application Controls (*Continued*)

MANUAL WORKAROUNDS

- Manual workarounds should be avoided in new systems being developed
- There should be one repository (e.g., one spreadsheet) for all manual workaround processes
- All transactions subject to the manual workaround process should be accounted for (e.g., reconciliations)

REJECTED TRANSACTIONS

- Rejected transactions should be aged and periodically reviewed to ensure the corrective action is taken in a timely manner

Test Analysis Report

The test analysis report:

- Documents the test analysis results and findings.
- Presents the demonstrated capabilities and deficiencies, including the security evaluation report needed for certification of the ERP system.
- Provides a basis for preparing a statement of ERP system readiness for implementation.

In a test analysis report:

- The system is certified independently using actual data, for its technical adequacy in meeting the predefined security requirements.
- Documented test results and a comparison of actual versus expected results should be included. There should also be an assessment that the system is operating effectively and is ready to be installed.
- Any caveats or restrictions are provided at this time.

The Risk Analysis

The following points apply to a risk analysis:

- The risk analysis should be reviewed and updated as necessary during each phase of the ERPLC to assure that no

new vulnerabilities have emerged and that appropriate
security measures have been installed.

- During the ERP security and certification reviews, audits
  should use the findings and recommendations of the risk
  analysis.
- The risk analysis should be prepared and maintained as a
  separate document. It should be reviewed and updated as
  necessary whenever the operational ERP system or operating
  environment are modified.

Note: All specifications should be sufficiently precise to allow
tests to be designed that verify that the requirements were
satisfied.

Training

One of the biggest mistakes businesses make is forgetting that employees must adapt to a new ERP system. Employees must be trained how
to operate the system and how to apply it to familiar tasks such as looking up and entering data. Furthermore, a new ERP system almost always means changes to business processes. That requires change
management to teach employees about new business practices and
manage staff reorganization. Employees often resent and resist change
when it means they have to change established work habits and take up
new reporting relationships. Despite all the money spent, an ERP deployment can fall flat on its face or operate at vastly reduced efficiency
if the company fails to adequately train the staff and effectively manage
the change.

Training manuals should:

- Describe the functions performed by the software in non-IT
  terminology so that the user organization can determine its
  applicability, as well as when and how to use it.
- Serve as a reference document for initiation procedures,
  preparation of input data and parameters, and for
  interpretation of results.

- Provide a full description of the ERP system as well as a section on procedures and requirements, including those related to security, privacy, and internal controls.
- Describe error, recovery, and file query procedures and requirements.

Operations Manual

The operations manual should:

- Provide computer operations staff with a description of the ERP system and the operating environment so that the ERP system can be run.
- Include an overview of the ERP system organization, program inventory and file inventory, as well as a description of the runs and sections on non-routine procedures, remote operations, and security requirements.

Maintenance Manual

The maintenance manual provides the maintenance programmer with the information and source code necessary to understand the programs, their operating environment, and their maintenance procedures and security requirements.

> **Note:** In order to maintain separation of duties, operations staff should not have access to this manual.

Audit reviews and evaluates the testing process, and provides advice to the help ensure that the ERP systems:

- Carry out prescribed management policies and meet legal requirements.
- Will meet user needs.
- Possess built-in controls necessary to provide reasonable assurance of proper operation.

- Contain automated audit-tool capabilities, when appropriate, to assist in evaluating controls.
- Will operate in an efficient and economical manner to minimize costs.
- Provide the capability to trace a transaction from its initiation through all intermediate processing steps to the resulting financial/management reports, as well as back to its origin. This enables management and audit to review the system in operation, and provides reconstructibility.

Note: The above items provide audit with a comprehensive set of control objectives to work from to develop audit criteria in this setting.

PHASE V—IMPLEMENTATION

Implementation and Conversion Plan

The implementation and conversion plan serves as a tool for directing the implementation of the ERP system at locations other than the test site, after the full testing of the ERP system, including security and internal control features, has been completed. Parts of the plan directed toward users should be presented in non-technical language. The plan should:

- Implement the approved operational plan, including extension/installation at other sites.
- Continue approved operations.
- Budget adequately.
- Control all changes and maintain/modify the ERP during its remaining life.
- Use problem reporting, change requests, and other change control mechanisms to facilitate the systematic correction and evolution of the ERP systems.

The Risk Analysis

The following points apply to the risk analysis:

- The risk analysis should be reviewed and updated, as necessary, during each phase of the ERPLC to assure that no new vulnerabilities have emerged and that appropriate security measures have been installed.
- During the ERP security and certification reviews, audit should use the findings and recommendations of the risk analysis.
- The risk analysis should be prepared and maintained as a separate document, reviewed and updated as necessary, when modification is made to the operational ERP system or operating environment.

Keep in mind that:

- All specifications should be sufficiently precise so that tests can be designed to verify that the requirements were satisfied.
- Properly designed systems, with excellent control mechanisms, might have these controls bypassed or overridden by management direction. This frequently occurs immediately after implementation when systems are put into operation. These controls are often overridden to get the system operational and then forgotten after the system errors have been corrected.
- ERP systems have manual aspects (e.g., input origination, output disposition), and these, together with the ERP system controls, should also be reviewed in conjunction with the review for adequacy.

PHASE VI—POST-IMPLEMENTATION

Periodic performance measurement and evaluation activities are performed to ensure that the system continues to meet its requirements in a cost-effective manner in the context of a changing system environment. These reviews are conducted by the audit and/or quality assurance staff. Detailed information on this phase is the subject of Chapter 5.

Detailed Audit Testing

Audit should select those documents, and criteria within documents, that have a significant effect on the management decision to proceed with each of the phases mentioned above. Those items should be examined through additional audit examination. The recommended audit objectives to be evaluated, including audit tests and control techniques are detailed in Chapter 5.

Audit Results Reporting

The objective of each phase review is to determine whether the activities and deliverables for that phase are adequate. Deficiencies are reported along with recommendations to resolve them. Problems identified, with the potential impact of the variance determined in the detailed audit tests, should appear in the audit report. The audit report should be released prior to management's decision on whether to proceed (i.e., sign-off) with that phase of the ERPLC.

Conclusion

Although ERP projects are complex and expensive, when properly implemented, they are worthwhile. Once fully deployed, the median annual savings from a new ERP system is estimated at $1.6 million per year. But every ERP system must be continually maintained and upgraded to take advantage of new applications, technologies, and features. ERP software is hardly static; there are major new developments as software grows to embrace the Internet and as companies open up their data and business processes to partners.

It is ERP software and the business process it describes—not the computing hardware—that lies at the real center of corporate information technology. This leads to change management, discussed in the next chapter.

Appendix 3A

Project Definition and Requirements Analysis Phase Audit Tests

CONTROL OBJECTIVES	AUDIT TEST	CONTROL TECHNIQUES
1. User Needs Statement clearly defines the need/problem and justification for ERP implementation for that need.	1. Determine that the user organizations have been identified.	Compare organizations identified in the Needs Statement with the Corporation organization chart to ensure that all appropriate users have been identified in the Needs Statement. Compare the Needs Statement to the appropriate user organization mission to ensure that the need serves the mission.
	2. Determine that the description of the need is in written form and includes the following expression of need in terms of user mission: a. Description of current function. b. Deficiencies of current function. c. Resources expended on the current function. d. Volumes of work produced with the current function, including peak processing performance plus projected growth.	User satisfaction questionnaire to identified users to verify the existence of deficiencies/problems/needs in the current system. Ensure the user Needs Statement adequately justified the need.

CONTROL OBJECTIVES	AUDIT TEST	CONTROL TECHNIQUES
	e. Statutory/regulatory mandates. f. Internal control/security requirements. g. Justification for improvement and changes. h. Scope and objectives of proposed system. i. Alternative solutions to solving the need. j. Interrelationships with other systems. k. Relationship with long-range plans and other information technology initiatives.	
2. User department's management should participate in the project initiation phase.	1. Review appropriate documentation to validate user participation such as: a. Minutes of steering committee meeting for evidence of user department management participation.	Locate appropriate documents and assess the reasonableness of user management participation.

(continued)

CONTROL OBJECTIVES	AUDIT TEST	CONTROL TECHNIQUES
	b. Review the project plans to determine the nature and extent of user department participation. c. Review user management to determine management's budgets for time allocation to efforts related to the project.	
	2. Interview user management to determine its understanding and level of participation in the project.	Structured interview techniques.
3. The feasibility study document should be clearly defined and documented.	1. Determine that the objectives and problem statement of the project have been described so that the objectives may serve as measurements of ERP systems effectiveness during and after the ERP system implementation.	Evaluate each objective from the perspective of whether or not that objective could be used in an in-process audit during ERP system implementation and in a post-implementation review to measure whether or not the system has achieved its objectives. Also relate the ERP system objectives back to the Needs Statement.

CONTROL OBJECTIVES	AUDIT TEST	CONTROL TECHNIQUES
	2. Determine that the analysis of alternatives is well documented. a. Verify there is a list of all identified alternatives and a description of how each alternative will alleviate the problem. b. Confirm with the user that no reasonable alternatives were omitted from the study. c. Verify that the alternatives are described in sufficient detail to adequately support the time and cost estimates, cost/benefit analyses, and impact studies. This is to challenge the reasons for selecting or rejecting alternatives. d. Verify that the analyses of the alternatives described in c. above apply comparable criteria in a consistent manner.	Ensure that the alternatives include, at a minimum, its information and analysis. If possible, the ERPLC methodology should be used.

(continued)

CONTROL OBJECTIVES	AUDIT TEST	CONTROL TECHNIQUES
	e. Verify that the alternatives are technologically feasible considering the level of the technical knowledge of the organization, and the level of sophistication of the proposed alternatives.	
	f. Verify that the alternatives meet user requirements.	
	g. Verify that the alternatives reflect official standards.	
	3. Determine that a technological feasibility study was prepared and documented for each alternative and that the technology is feasible, considering the technical sophistication existent or available through the organization.	
	a. Review the technological Feasibility Study report to see if it has adequately addressed:	
	i. Hardware needs and availability.	
	ii. System software needs and availability.	
	iii. Communications hardware and software needs and availability.	

CONTROL OBJECTIVES	CONTROL AUDIT TEST	TECHNIQUES
	iv. Valid time constraints in the user department's information requirements and the manner of satisfying them.	
	v. Operational feasibility, such as whether the new project fits into the current mix of hardware, software, and communications environment.	
	vi. Feasibility study assumptions and constraints.	
	vii. The criteria used for the feasibility study.	
	b. Review the technological feasibility study report to see if it has considered:	
	i. Legal considerations related to inter-state or international transfer of data	
	ii. Regulating constraints related to the use of technology and the manner of securing regulating authority's consurrence or approval	

(continued)

CONTROL OBJECTIVES	AUDIT TEST	CONTROL TECHNIQUES
	iii. Verify that there is a consensus among user departments and designers concerning the technological aspects of the system's configuration.	
	iv. Determine the organizational capability to manage the related technologies and whether the technologies would potentially be operated and maintained in-house or contracted out.	
	v. Confirm with independent sources the reliability and track record of the recommended hardware and software.	
	4. Determine that the recommended course of action is adequately substantiated as the most feasible.	
	5. Determine that:	
	a. Options/alternatives were considered.	
	b. Specified modifications were made.	
	c. Contractual provisions were met.	

CONTROL OBJECTIVES	AUDIT TEST	CONTROL TECHNIQUES
4. ERP System control and security vulnerabilities should have been determined, as well as the magnitude of associated threats	1. Determine that a risk management team has been formed, that it included the appropriate individuals, and evaluate the reasonableness of the following risk team tasks: a. Review the list of identified vulnerabilities. b. Verify that the magnitude of each vulnerability has been stated. c. Verify that the vulnerabilities address all aspects of the ERP application, including tele-communication links, contingency planning, and so forth. d. Verify that all known risks in existent systems are fully considered. e. Verify that recommended safeguards are included in the design to address the identified risks.	To evaluate reasonableness of the results, assess the makeup of the risk management team, the performance of that team through the documented minutes and reports, the methodology used, and the completeness of the results against a generally accepted vulnerabilities and risk analysis methodology, such as the ERPLC, described in this book.

(continued)

CONTROL OBJECTIVES	AUDIT TEST	CONTROL TECHNIQUES
5. Cost/benefit analysis should include all of the cost and benefit considerations associated with the initiation, operations, and maintenance of the ERP.	1. Determine that the analysis of the project costs and benefits was prepared to evaluate the economic feasibility of each alternative. a. Review the summary of present systems costs as well as estimated costs of each alternative to ascertain that all costs have been included in the summary. b. Evaluate assumptions and constraints in the cost/benefit analysis for reasonableness. c. Verify that user and system costs cover all phases of the ERPLC. d. Verify that estimated costs for an alternative include hardware and software enhancements needed to support that alternative. e. Verify that the basis of estimation and computation of costs appear to be reasonable.	Compare the type and extent of cost/benefit information developed during the project to the categories of cost/benefit information included in such documents. Ensure that the information has been summarized in a manner consistent with that specified in documents. Ensure the cost/benefit analysis provides adequate information.

CONTROL OBJECTIVES	AUDIT TEST	CONTROL TECHNIQUES
	f. Verify that benefits are quantified where possible. g. Verify there is a substantial consensus among end users, and implementors concerning system costs, benefits, and contractual requirements. h. Verify that the benefits claimed appear to be reasonable.	
6. Management should review the feasibility study reports and decide whether to proceed. When the decision is made to proceed, one of the alternatives should be selected as the starting point for the following ERP system implementation phases.	1. Verify that the system decision paper has been disseminated to all user management for analysis and approval. 2. Verify that the paper is approved by the CIO.	Structured interview technique. Compare the documented management decision on the ERP to the system decision paper to verify that the alternative selected is included in the system decision paper.
	3. Verify that the decision is made to proceed with the ERP, that the alternative selected is the one included in the system decision paper.	

(continued)

CONTROL OBJECTIVES	CONTROL AUDIT TEST	TECHNIQUES
7. Validate that an analysis was made prior to implementation to determine whether the work could have been done more economically through in-house staffing and/or the use of consultants.	Review the documentation in the phase to determine that alternate means of customizing ERP were given adequate consideration.	Structured interview—Meet with involved personnel to validate documents and confirm that appropriate consideration was given to alternate implementation methods.

Appendix 3B

External and Internal Design Phases Audit Tests

CONTROL OBJECTIVES	AUDIT TEST	CONTROL TECHNIQUES
1. A project plan should be developed that specifies the strategy for managing the ERP implementation.	1. Validate that the attributes included within the project plan are accurate and complete.	Review the project plan attributes.
	2. Determine that the plan identifies the strategy for managing the implementation effort.	Use project plan checklists.
	3. Determine that the plan identifies goals and activities for all phases and subphases, and includes milestone dates and resource estimates.	Compare the attributes of the project plan to other projects of equal size and complexity to validate reasonableness of estimates and milestones.
2. A definition of existing and new information requirements should be specified with exacting detail.	1. Determine whether the existing and new information requirements are complete and specified in enough detail to permit test data generation in subsequent phases for compliance verification.	Verify the information attributes in the functional requirements document to the definitions in the data dictionary.
	2. Interview appropriate user personnel to validate reasonableness of information requirements. Determine the constraints on the data requirements. Indicate the limits of the data requirements with respect to further expansion	

CONTROL OBJECTIVES	AUDIT TEST	CONTROL TECHNIQUES
	of utilization, especially emphasizing the constraints that could prove critical during the ERP implementation process.	
	3. Validate that the information requirements are complete and consistent with standard ERP processing definitions.	
	4. Ascertain if the description of the present system is adequate and serviceable as a basis for studying the needs for the proposed ERP system. Determine if the areas in the present system which would be changed by the proposed ERP system have been clearly identified.	Review audit workpapers of previous audits indicating the attributes of the system being automated or changed. Interview those responsible for operating and maintaining the current system for their perspectives on current problems and the proposed system's impact on the current system and its interface systems.
	5. Include audit tests to ensure that functional requirements are considered.	Use items enumerated under the functional requirements document obtained from the project team.

(continued)

CONTROL OBJECTIVES	AUDIT TEST	CONTROL TECHNIQUES
3. All input requirements should be defined and documented.	1. Review the adequacy of documentation for input require-ments of the new ERP system to ensure they include: a. Editing and validation requirements. b. Input or update authorization. c. Establishment of appropriate control totals. d. Required precision for each quantitative field. e. Time requirements for the entry of transactions. f. Requirements for handling inaccurate error identification/correction or incomplete data. g. Rules for authorizing each of the key transactions. h. Verification that the individuals identified by the authorization rules have been granted that specific authority.	Validate input requirements specifications to data dictionary specifications. Interview users responsible for data items to confirm accuracy and completeness of input requirements. Validate attributes of data to that specified by appropriate regulations.

CONTROL OBJECTIVES	AUDIT TEST	CONTROL TECHNIQUES
	i. The retention requirements for input data (automated and hard copy) have been specified. j. Online entry application considerations. k. Suspense files—verify their use. l. System override/by-pass—verify that controls over these transactions are specified and limited. m. Describe input forms/transactions/sources/volume. n. Input terminal/device specifications. o. Input technology/compatibility.	
4. Output requirements should be defined and documented.	1. Review the adequacy of documentation for output requirements of the new ERP system to ensure that the provisions include such items as: a. Content and format of reports and screens generated. b. Authorization of users to receive reports. c. Retention period of reports. d. Provision of audit trails and sufficiency of information to trace/validate accuracy.	Interview users to validate the accuracy and completeness of the output requirements. Develop user satisfaction questionnaire. ERP implementation methodology review questionnaires (if included as part of the ERP implementation methodology). If checklists are not provided by the ERP implementation methodology, the auditor should

(continued)

CONTROL OBJECTIVES	CONTROL AUDIT TEST	TECHNIQUES
	e. Retention periods for outputs (automated and hard copy). f. The ability to ensure control of the completeness, accuracy, and authorization of data. g. Purpose of the report.	develop them, as appropriate, for review purposes.
5. Specification for processing steps should be defined and documented.	1. Review processing specifications to determine if they are adequate and were prepared in accordance with management policies, to assure that: a. Cut-off methods have been established. b. All ERP-generated transactions have been identified. c. Appropriate authority exists for generating ERP transactions. d. Requirements specify method for monitoring the ERP-generated transactions. e. The methods required for maintaining independent control totals on key fields are reasonable.	Processing review checklist (if provided by the ERP implementation methodology). If checklists are not provided by the ERP implementation methodology, the auditor should develop them. Interview users to validate the accuracy and completeness of the processing specifications. System modeling/prototyping to produce simulated system results for validation by end users of the reasonableness and usefulness of those results in user processing.

CONTROL OBJECTIVES	AUDIT TEST	CONTROL TECHNIQUES
	f. Control totals will be supportable and the transactions comprising the control totals can be identified.	
6. A plan for converting from existing process to new process has been documented.	1. Review conversion plan for: a. Controls during conversion. b. Handling of pipeline transactions. are in place and conform to agency policies and procedures.	Interview key user and ERP processing personnel to ensure appropriate conversation processes
7. The impact of ERP system failures should be defined and reconstruction requirements specified.	1. Determine if a decision has been made about the necessity of recovering the ERP system in the event of failure; and if so, whether the requirements for retention, reconstruction, and/or alternate processing procedures have been defined. 2. Simulated disaster scenario—key security personnel/operations personnel can simulate potential disasters and then determine, based on the system specification, whether the available information	Interview security officers/ operations personnel to determine whether they believe reconstruction requirements are adequate. Determine that the retention period for reconstructions is consistent with retention period specified in appropriate laws, regulations, and organization retention programs.

(continued)

CONTROL OBJECTIVES	AUDIT TEST	CONTROL TECHNIQUES
	would be necessary for reconstruction purposes. (Note that in later phases actual disasters can be simulated.)	
8. The level of service necessary to achieve the processing objective should be defined and documented.	1. Determine that: a. A desired percentage of uptime has been specified. b. The response time for each transaction has been specified. c. The needed computer capacity has been specified. d. It is reasonable based upon user department needs.	Interview key user personnel to validate that the specified service levels are adequate. Interview key operations personnel to validate that operation can provide the processing necessary to accomplish the desired service levels.
9. The internal control and security requirements should be defined and documented.	Determine whether the user requirements include security, control, and privacy issues and then validate that those requirements are adequate and address previously defined risks.	Identify the control techniques needed to minimize vulnerabilities for the proposed system. Compliance with the requirements.
10. The user requirements should identify critical/sensitive data and assets, and how those items should be controlled during ERP processing.	Validate that the system requirements indicate the data and asset sensitivity/criticality protection requirements.	Review appropriate legislation (e.g., in USA, Privacy Act of 1974, Freedom of Information Act, etc.) in order to validate that the types of transactions/data/assets governed by the system will be adequately protected.

CONTROL OBJECTIVES	AUDIT TEST	CONTROL TECHNIQUES
11. Audit and quality assurance tools and techniques should be planned for the system.	Validate that needed audit and quality assurance tools and techniques are available in the system or, if they are missing, develop requirements for these tools and techniques.	Review appropriate documentation and interview cognizant personnel.
12. The system decision paper should include all of the information needed by user management to make a decision on action to be taken regarding the ERP system.	1. Verify there is a consensus among user departments and designers concerning the recommended alternative, the costs/benefits, and the technological aspect of the systems implementation approach. 2. Determine that the system decision paper includes all of the essential information on the ERP system, such as: a. Mission need. b. Risks. c. Alternatives. d. Costs/benefits. e. Management plan. f. Supporting rationale for decisions.	Conduct structured interviews. Compare the structure and content of the system decision paper to standard business practices.

(continued)

CONTROL OBJECTIVES	AUDIT TEST	CONTROL TECHNIQUES
	g. Affordability in terms of projected budget and out-year funding.	
	h. Conceptual definitions.	
	i. Practicality of implementation plan.	
	• ERPLC	
	• Team/personnel/resources	
	• Monitoring/oversight	
	j. Consistency with long-range plans and other key initiatives.	

Appendix 3C

Pre-implementation Phase

CONTROL OBJECTIVES	AUDIT TEST	CONTROL TECHNIQUES
1. The revised project plan is current and provides the direction needed to effectively and efficiently manage the project.	1. Confirm with the project manager that the plan is up to date, is being followed, and provides adequate information to adjust project direction to ensure the project will be completed on time, within budget, and produce the expected deliverables.	Compare the status of completed documents as included in the project plan. Verify that the plan is accurate, and, through interview with the document developers, ensure that problems in their work are appropriately addressed by project management.
2. The final system design should be approved by all appropriate levels of management as meeting all predetermined needs.	1. Determine that user department management, and other appropriate management, have reviewed the external/internal design specifications/documents. 2. Confirm that user department management has approved the design as meeting their needs.	Manual examination of evidence indicating that the material had been reviewed (e.g., reviewing minutes of meeting, department memorandum, departmental time sheets, etc.) Examine user "signoff" of design phase documents. System development scheduling software—obtain status information from the scheduling packages.
3. Sufficient ERP processing and security controls should be incorporated in the detailed design to ensure the integrity of the system.	Review the detailed design specifications and identify the system controls to be built in the system to evaluate the adequacy of those controls. (Note: If control documentation	Risk points are where controls should be placed. The auditor has a variety of strategies available to identify risk points. The adequacy of controls should be addressed at

CONTROL OBJECTIVES	AUDIT TEST	CONTROL TECHNIQUES
	does not exist within the system design documents, this can be an extremely time-consuming task for the auditor.) The areas to be addressed are: 1. How are the controls specified in requirements designed into system? 2. What new risks does design introduce and what control reduce risk? 3. What mechanisms have been designed to ensure ongoing integrity (e.g., exception reports, control total comparisons)? 4. What are the access control mechanisms?	those points. If the system has been designed using structured design, then the nodes in the structure indicate the points where controls should be exercised. The auditor can use the structured design to show the data flow in the points where data should be controlled. The controls can be documented on the structured design, with the absence of control at the nodes of the structure indicating potential control weakness. If controls are not documented, and the system is not designed using a structured method, the auditor has the option of selecting one or more of the control design methodologies available through the private or public sector. If emphasis is on the security part of control, then refer to security assessment methodology and practices.

(continued)

CONTROL OBJECTIVES	AUDIT TEST	CONTROL TECHNIQUES
4. Rules for authorizing transactions should be defined and documented.	1. Determine that the method for authorizing each transaction has been documented, and that the method is reasonable. (Note that the audit process for this will vary depending on whether the transaction originates on paper or electronically.)	For paper transactions, use a structured interview technique to validate that all transactions have been identified, and that the rules for authorizing those transactions are defined. Note that, for financial systems, the financial officer should indicate how financial transactions are authorized. For automated transactions, the auditor needs to use the structured interviewing techniques to ensure that all the electronically originated transactions have been identified. The assessment over the controls for authorization is normally implemented through security access packages. The auditor should validate that those security software packages, or equivalent, will be used to validate the authorization of transactions.

CONTROL OBJECTIVES	AUDIT TEST	CONTROL TECHNIQUES
5. Documentation suitable for use as audit trails should be incorporated into the Internal Design.	1. Verify that the audit trail specifications include both the manual and automated segments, and that the audit trail is adequate to trace transactions from point of origin (source documents) to control totals, and from control totals back to supporting transactions. 2. Determine whether sufficient generations of documentation will be stored away from the primary site, so that processing can be reconstructed if the primary site is destroyed. Validate that the documentation will be retained for the correct retention period based on federal programs, regulations, and agency policy.	The auditor should prepare a document flow diagram. The objective of the document flow diagram is to pictorially show the flow of documents, including electronic documents, who is responsible for those documents, and where the documents are stored. The specific audit trail would be illustrated through notation on the document flow diagram, and references to the specific documents, both manual and electronic. Review of computer operations prepared disaster plan. This plan will indicate what documents are to be stored away from the primary site, where they will be stored, and the length of storage. The plan should also indicate how and when the disaster procedures have been tested to validate that they work.

(continued)

CONTROL OBJECTIVES	AUDIT TEST	CONTROL TECHNIQUES
		Use structured interview techniques to identify correct retention periods and compare that to system documentation.
6. A vulnerability assessment should be planned and performed in accordance with generally accepted criteria.	1. Determine that a vulnerability assessment has been planned, performed, and documented. 2. Review the vulnerability assessment for reasonableness.	Use structured interview techniques to validate with involved parties (refer to identified responsible participant for security) the completeness of the vulnerability assessment.
7. The system/subsystem, program and database specifications should provide the correct architectural solution to meet the documented requirements from the definition phase.	Ensure that the documented system solution will provide the information needed to meet the objectives defined in the previous phases. Review the system/subsystem, program, and database specifications document contents.	Technical peer review group—A team of peers can be established to review the design to ensure that it meets the system requirements. The auditor may be a member of that review team, with specific responsibilities for the adequacy of the design of the system of internal controls and security procedures. Use the system/subsystem, program, and database specifications document concerns.

CONTROL OBJECTIVES	AUDIT TEST	CONTROL TECHNIQUES
8. The security and internal control related specifications should provide controls adequate for satisfying the control requirements defined in the previous phase.	Ensure that the documented security and internal control specifications satisfy the controls defined in the previous phase.	Use the items enumerated under the security and internal control related specifications document.
9. A validation, verification, and testing plan should be developed and documented.	1. Review the validation, verification, and testing plan and specifications to ensure that it includes all of the important parts. 2. Verify that the test plan adequately validates the system requirements defined in the previous phase.	Compare the information included within the test plan against test plan standards and guides. Prepare a function/test matrix. This matrix should be specified and, if included within the documentation, audit need only ensure that the function/ test matrix is complete. This matrix lists all of the application functions (i.e., requirements) on one axis of the matrix and then cross-references it to all of the tests included in the test plan. This provides proof that the test plan is complete.

(continued)

CONTROL OBJECTIVES	AUDIT TEST	CONTROL TECHNIQUES
10. Assure that audit and quality assurance tools and techniques have been included in the internal design documents.	Validate that the needed audit and quality assurance tools and techniques have been included in the system as it is designed.	Review appropriate documentation and interview cognizant personnel.
11. Assure that the ERP system has optimized the use of technology.	Validate that the ERP system effectively uses technology and that adequate controls are incorporatedinto the system to control technology.	Compare the technology controls against the control for technology in the appropriate part of the ERP systems manual. Determine that the test plan for the ERP includes adequate tests of technology. (Note: If audit does not feel qualified to evaluate technology, consideration should be given to engaging a consultant to evaluate the effective use of technology.)
12. Ensure that the system decision continues to be supported.	Ensure that the system decision paper has been updated.	Obtain and review a copy of the updated system decision paper or its equivalent
13. Program documentation and programming standards should be enforced to ensure that documentation is maintained in accordance	Review project documents to ensure they include procedures for compliance with organization's procedures, standards and policies.	Structured interview— Validate through project personnel how they ensure compliance to the appropriate standards and policies.

CONTROL OBJECTIVES	AUDIT TEST	CONTROL TECHNIQUES
	Review completed documents for compliance to standards and policies.	ERPLC methodology review checklist—The ERPLC methodologies may provide checklists for use in reviewing compliance to the methodology and appropriate procedures and standards.
14. Each program should have adequate test data prepared to validate the functioning of the executable source code.	Create sufficient test data to validate the important functions of the ERP.	Test data—Process generated test data to validate the adequacy of program/system internal controls. Program test matrix—Prepare a matrix which tests data elements on one axis and all valid and invalid types of data on the other. Assure that all valid and invalid combinations of data have been tested. Application software analysis—Create a flow chart/map from the source code to validate the functioning of the program.

(continued)

CONTROL OBJECTIVES	AUDIT TEST	CONTROL TECHNIQUES
15. Each program should include a detailed narrative description of the processing to be performed and the logic of that processing. (Note that documentation may be included within the program, maintained on electronic media outside the program, or may be prepared manually.)	1. Review the detailed narrative prepared as part of the program documentation, and determine that it conforms to the original system definition narrative, and that it is adequate for understanding and maintenance purposes. 2. Determine if there is an understandable "link" between the code and the supporting requirements.	Generalized audit software—Packages provide routines which will analyze data and extract from production files a representative number of records for test purposes. ERPLC methodology checklist may include checklists for reviewing the adequacy of program documentation, and its consistency with system documentation. Quality control/quality assurance review—if an independent group within ERP processing performs a review of this type, audit can evaluate the review documentation to determine whether that review can be relied upon as a test of performance for this audit objective. Peer review—Another programmer can review a program to ensure the accuracy and completeness of the program documentation.

CONTROL OBJECTIVES	AUDIT TEST	CONTROL TECHNIQUES
		Documentation software packages—Certain software packages automatically generate the documentation needed to understand individual source programs or groups of programs, including graphic record layouts. Because documentation is in a standardized format, it only requires minimal training to understand the structure and content of that documentation. Audit can use it to evaluate the program functionality.
16. All of the source codes should be executed during testing.	1. Determine that all of the executable lines of source codes have been exercised during testing. 2. Validate that all of the functions specified for the program have been incorporated into the program.	Mapping/tracing—Use a package that will count the source codes exercised during testing. The programs should include all of the functions described in the program specification. Program test matrix—Prepare a matrix which lists the program functions on one axis of the matrix and the program requirements on the other axis of the matrix. Then cross-reference in the matrix the implemented function to the functional specifications.

(continued)

CONTROL OBJECTIVES	AUDIT TEST	CONTROL TECHNIQUES
17. Run manuals for operators' use should be prepared and adequately documented in an operations manual.	Assure that the operator manuals are in compliance with documentation standards, and that they include for each job step the following information: a. Program function. b. Hardware requirements. c. Explanation of all console messages together with appropriate operator response. d. Output creation and its disposition. e. Proper identification of output file labels. f. Appropriate restart or notification procedures specified for error or failure conditions. g. Checkpoint controls for proper run-to-run control.	Operator run manual checklist—Checklists should be available in the ERPLC methodology that indicate the contents of the operator manual.
18. A maintenance manual should be prepared with adequate information on projected maintenance needs and problems.	Review the maintenance manual for projected a. periodic software needs. b. periodic hardware needs. c. possible problem areas.	Use information found in the ERPLC methodology for appropriate information to be found in the maintenance manual.

CONTROL OBJECTIVES	AUDIT TEST	CONTROL TECHNIQUES
19. Manuals for users should be prepared and adequately documented.	Verify that user manuals exist which include the documentation specified by the ERP standards, and assure that, for each user manual, documentation includes the following: a. Specifications and layout for input data. b. Need for control totals. c. Manner of submitting data. d. Manner of receiving outputs. e. Manner of querying the system. f. Responsibility for converting data into machine-readable form. g. Responsibility for resolving errors or other inaccuracies. h. Parameter for priority assignment for processing remote job entry (RJE) type work.	User manual checklist—Checklists should be available in the ERPLC methodology that indicate the contents of the user manual.
20. A training plan should be prepared and documented in detail. This may be found within or based upon the user manual and the operations/maintenance manual.	1. Determine whether a written training plan has been prepared. 2. Confirm with user department management that the training plan anticipates its needs adequately.	Training plan checklist—ERPLC methodology and/or ERP standards should identify what attributes should be included within the training plan.

(continued)

CONTROL OBJECTIVES	AUDIT TEST	CONTROL TECHNIQUES
		Use structured interview—Inquire of user management regarding the adequacy of the training plan.
21. Determine that good programming practices have been employed to take advantage of modern software engineering and computer efficiencies.	1. Determine whether the ERP has been written in accordance with ERP processing standards and procedures. 2. Use software packages to analyze the efficiency of program code.	Programs should contain checklists of standards complied with and not complied with. Programs may be reviewed by the quality assurance function to verify compliance to standards. There are software packages that can be used to measure the efficiency of operation.
22. Each program should be tested to ensure that it correctly performs the functions assigned to that unit.	1. Validate that there is at least one test condition for each program function. 2. Ensure that there has been adequate coverage of program instructions during the test.	Examine the test plan to determine that each function has been defined, and that there is a test condition to evaluate that function. There are software packages that can be used to count the instructions exercised during tests to validate whether an adequate coverage of the code has been exercised during testing.

CONTROL OBJECTIVES	CONTROL AUDIT TEST	TECHNIQUES
23. An implementation and conversion plan should be prepared and adequately documented.	Verify that the implementation and conversion plan has been produced and satisfies concerns.	Use the implementation and conversion plan checklist.
24. An updated system decision paper should have been produced at the start of this phase.	Verify that an updated system decision paper has been produced and is backed up by new information developed at the end of the last phase.	Review the document. Use structured interviews of responsible participants.
25. A change control process should be in place for the user manual and the operations/maintenance manual.	Verify that a change control process has been defined and is implemented in terms of timing criteria and responsible personnel.	Use structured interviews to confirm that such a change control process is in place.
26. Unit, module, and integration testing should be conducted according to the test plan and applicable ERP test standards.	Validate that the tests conducted are the tests included in the updated test plan.	Test plan/test checklist—The tests indicated in the test plan should be traced to the actual tests conducted to validate that the planned tests have been performed. Test standards checklist should be used to validate that testing was performed in conjunction with the standards.

(continued)

127

CONTROL OBJECTIVES	AUDIT TEST	CONTROL TECHNIQUES
27. Test results should be evaluated by data processing management and by user department management to determine that the system functions properly.	1. Review test documentation and verify that predetermined results were developed in advance, were compared with test results, and the two were in agreement. 2. Validate that user management evaluated the test results. 3. Determine that generally accepted requirements for certification of controls have been met.	Comparison packages—A number of software packages permit comparisons of expected results against actual results. Structured interview—Audit needs to interview user personnel to ensure they have performed the steps necessary to validate the correctness of test results.
28. Test results should be recorded and retained as part of the system documentation.	Examine all documentation related to the testing process and assess its completeness; then verify that responsibility for retaining and updating documentation relating to system testing has been properly assigned.	Test documentation checklist are included in the ongoing system documentation.
29. Circumstances under which a parallel run of both existing and new systems is considered desirable should be identified, and criteria for its termination should be stated.	Determine whether user department management's decision to require a parallel run before acceptance test is cost/benefit justified, and if so that it was performed in accordance with criteria established in advance.	Test results comparison—A variety of software packages will compare the results of two parallel runs, without losing the ability to compare when one or two unequal conditions occur.

CONTROL OBJECTIVES	AUDIT TEST	CONTROL TECHNIQUES
30. An updated conversion plan should be prepared to include assignment of individual responsibilities.	1. Ascertain that both the user department and the ERP processing department have reviewed and approved the updated conversion plan; and that the conversion plan is documented.	Conversion plan checklist should include a checklist of the attributes that are to be included in conversion plans. Audit can use this to validate the existence of the appropriate attributes of a conversion plan. Audit should evaluate the accuracy of conversion of programs and data, using generalized audit software to validate correctness of conversion.
31. Ensure that adequate provisions have been made to assure continuity of processing.	1. Verify that the following tests have been done: a. Backup and recovery. b. Capacity/stress test. c. Planned failure tests. d. Contingency plan tests.	
32. Determine that a security evaluation certification, and an accreditation have been performed and appropriate documents and statements prepared.	1. Examine the security certification and accreditation statements.	Use guidelines on security evaluation, certification, and accreditation.

(continued)

CONTROL OBJECTIVES	AUDIT TEST	CONTROL TECHNIQUES
33. Determine that the implementation and conversion plan has been updated and currently represents the current status of the ERP.	Verify that the implementation and conversion plan contains all the necessary attributes, and that those attributes are accurate and current.	Use the implementation and conversion plan document checklist from the phase in which this document was prepared, and then verify the information in the user manual against the appropriate evaluation and acceptance documentation to validate the accuracy and currency of this document.
34. Determine that the user manual has been updated and currently represents the current status of the ERP.	Verify that the user manual contains all the necessary attributes, and that those attributes are accurate and current.	Use the user manual document checklist from the phase in which this document was prepared, and then verify the information in the user manual against the appropriate evaluation and acceptance documentation to validate the accuracy and currency of this document.
35. Determine that the operations/maintenance manual has been updated and currently represents the current status of the ERP.	Verify that the operations/maintenance manual contains all the necessary attributes, and that those attributes are accurate and current.	Use the operations/maintenance manual checklist from the phase in which this document was prepared, and then verify the information in the operations/maintenance manual

CONTROL OBJECTIVES	AUDIT TEST	CONTROL TECHNIQUES
		against the appropriate evaluation and acceptance documentation to validate the accuracy and currency of this document.
36. Determine that the project plan has been updated and represents the current status of the ERP.	Verify that the project plan contains all the necessary attributes, that those attributes are accurate and current.	Use the project plan document checklist from the phase in which this document was prepared, and then verify the information in the project plan against the appropriate evaluation and acceptance documentation to validate the accuracy and currency of this document.
37. Determine that the system decision paper has been updated and represents the current status of the ERP.	Verify that the system decision paper contains all the necessary attributes, and that those attributes are accurate and current.	Use the system decision paper checklist from the phase in which this document was prepared, and verify the information in the systems decision paper against the appropriate evaluation and acceptance documentation to validate the accuracy and currency of this document.

4

Change Management

CHANGE MANAGEMENT PROCESSES

The *legitimacy* of the programs included in ERP software is a key factor in the validity of the data generated by the ERP system. It is critical that any changes to these programs are executed in a controlled environment.

Organizations develop and deploy ERP systems to support their business needs. Since these needs will change over time, it is critical that organizations have the ability to adapt to changing business requirements. Organizations should establish a production change management framework to achieve this.

The analysis of existing production change request processes and requirements determines change management requirements. Questionnaires, one-to-one interviews and analysis of existing processes obtain information. In addition to interviewing key personnel within the ERP system group, interviews are conducted with organizations that interface with the ERP system group.

Organizations do what they can to manage change with the information and tools available to them. There should not be different change management processes within an organization. There should be a single change management process dedicated to a common business focus.

Without a singular business focus, a number of different processes are bound to be used based on specific departmental viewpoints and disconnects will invariably occur. Inconsistent and undocumented communication about change leads to confusion, lower efficiency, and lower productivity.

Here are some audit control red flags for a change management framework:

- There is no overall change management framework.   Absence of a process for change management across all organizations results in:
  - No process for supporting change through the entire change request life cycle, resulting in late notifications to all impacted parties, causing bottlenecks and delays.
  - Unplanned or informal change management activities resulting in service-level inconsistencies and insufficient impact analysis.
- Lack of a centralized repository in which to track change:
  - Inability to view all change activity throughout an organization to lessen the impact on the environment and the client.
  - Inability to properly plan similar changes across an organization, resulting in a lost opportunity to achieve economy of scale.
- Lack of formal communication from development organizations to support organizations and vice versa, regarding development projects and infrastructure changes. This increases the risk of errors and increases the cost of support.
- Lack of a process by which the ERP system group management can review, evaluate, and plan infrastructure development to reduce costs while providing their clients with required processing capabilities and infrastructure stability.

While these issues are not fatal, they prevent organizations from reaping the rewards of improved product quality, reduced support and infrastructure costs, and greater client satisfaction.

Methodology

Audit has to evaluate the production change request management process framework and identify areas for improvement. This section provides information on how to evaluate the change management process.

Change management is a continuous process comprised of four interconnected quadrants, or functional areas. These quadrants are:

1. Customer service (internal or external).
2. Change requests.
3. Implementation (i.e., implementing the change requests).
4. Deployment (i.e., deploying the change requests).

The change management system consists of the processes in these four quadrants, integrated, understood and managed.

A review of each quadrant and an analysis of the people, processes, and technologies in each of them will now be covered. See Exhibit 4.1.

Customer Service Requirements

Define what these requirements are. How are they defined and established?

Organizational Roles and Responsibilities

- Establish customer service roles, resources, and responsibilities for interfacing with the end-to-end change control process and system (e.g., change control board, change control tool, etc.).
- Establish roles/resources for recording and measuring metrics for compliance with service-level agreements (SLA).

Process Framework

- Implement a mechanism and process to record and review metrics for measuring compliance with service-level agreements (SLA) that are defined for trouble/requests reported to the help desk. Distribute reporting on these metrics for accountability.
- Implement a process for the help desk to notify requestors when tickets/requests are resolved and completed by support groups.

Exhibit 4.1   Change Management Quadrant

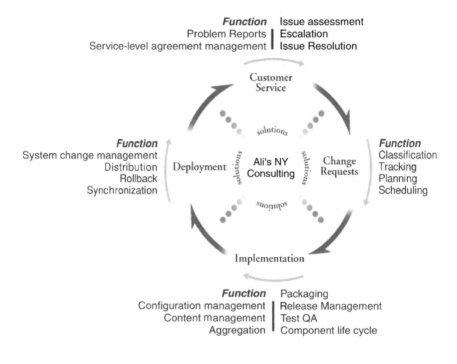

SLA – Service-Level Agreement

- Enforce and adequately communicate the process for support groups to always notify requestors and the help desk after a ticket has been resolved.
- Define and document a process to update known problems/common errors on an ongoing basis.
- Enforce and adequately communicate the process to submit all software/hardware/connectivity problems/requests through the help desk.
- Establish training for any new change management tools/processes implemented.

Change Request Requirements

These define how change requests are initiated, considered, authorized, and processed.

Organizational Roles and Responsibilities

- Establish a change control board. The board will review and evaluate all change requests to approve, prioritize, and schedule all changes affecting the ERP system group. Clarify guidelines on how changes are approved and prioritized for the change control board.
- Establish a clear line of functional responsibility for each type of change, detailing roles and responsibilities for each organization in the path of the change.
- Create a change management department responsible for managing the change request process that includes evaluating change risk, organizing a change event calendar, and chairing the change control board.

Process Framework

- Define and document the criteria for accepting emergency changes and the *fast path* process they will follow.
- Develop a change tracking process that defines appropriate roles and responsibilities. Include standardized documentation, verification, and approval steps.
- Map the systems impact and dependency for each type of change to eliminate possible collisions.
- Clearly document the organizations involved in every type of change; the method by which the change will be communicated between organizations; and the timeframes and content of that communication.
- Establish a process by which the impact of all changes will be evaluated and mitigated. This will reduce risk and eliminate unexpected outages.

- Define and standardize the information required for each type of change request to eliminate incorrect or incomplete change requirements. These can lead to miscommunication, imperfect impact analysis, and errors.

Technology

- Implement a change request and tracking tool to provide a centralized facility that records and tracks all change requests. Define views for all organizations impacted by change into the tool.
- Interface the change request system with any developed defect tracking tool or process.
- Select a change request tool with a simple-to-use standard interface that can record changes. Select a tool with a Web interface.
- Select a tool with a central repository that allows the ERP services group to view all impending changes and plan accordingly.
- Define and enforce required information for change requests within the tool.
- Establish training for any new change management tools/processes implemented.

Implementation Requirements

These define how changes are implemented in the active organization.

Organizational Roles and Responsibilities

- Establish which project-related items require signoff. Document who must sign the item and at what point the item must be signed. Store all signed documentation in a standardized and centrally located repository.
- Document, define, and enforce development test procedures and responsibilities.
- Document and share knowledge of all in-house and vendor applications with every IT group.

- Notify all support groups (network services, etc.) early in the change request process to perform an impact analysis regarding infrastructure effects like network performance.
- Store standard project plans in a centralized repository so that they can be tracked, prioritized, and scheduled.

Process Framework

- Implement a centralized defect tracking process that can prioritize defects.
- Define and document a hot-fix emergency change process that will quickly attend to high-priority changes.
- Establish a standard process to document service-level agreements.
- Document, define, and enforce development test procedures.
- Establish a standard mechanism/process to communicate the status of QA testing to the clients/users.
- Implement a formal process to communicate a change request to the help desk or application development groups.
- Define a formal hardware capacity planning process for the ERP system group to avoid potential performance issues.
- Document a standard baseline procedure for all project work products (documentation, project plans, application code, etc.)

Technology

- Implement a centralized defect-tracking tool to prioritize defects.
- Implement a tool to communicate a change request to the help desk or application development groups.
- Establish a collaboration tool that can share standardized project plans across the organization so that they can be tracked, prioritized, and scheduled.
- Establish training for any new change management tools/processes implemented in the ERP group system.

Deployment Requirements

These define how changes are deployed into the operating environment.

Organizational Roles and Responsibilities

- Define and document the relationships and distinctions between the infrastructure design responsibilities of systems architecture compared with other ERP system infrastructure support groups (e.g., systems engineering, network services, end user support, etc.). Draw clear lines of responsibility.
- Define and document business continuity requirements for software/hardware, and the responsibilities for ongoing disaster recovery/business continuity management/planning. Include a process to maintain, update, and communicate this information.

Process Framework for Deployment

- Design a standard process to perform cost benefit analysis of new technologies.
- Implement checkpoints where developers and ERP system signoff on requirements and design specifications. A consistent process for checkpoints will ensure that each development organization and ERP system group can assess the impact of proposed change and properly plan and schedule.
- Establish standard process to manage services and projects by third-party vendors. Formalize the day-to-day controls that are needed to meet production and deployment requirements.
- Create an infrastructure rollback procedure. Restore processes and scripts that need to be created and include all critical business requirements.
- Test deployment and restoration processes.
- Create, report, and monitor deployment and restoration metrics.
- Establish consistent lines for information exchange between all IT organizations (i.e., network services and systems engineering).

- Define and apply global infrastructure testing procedures as a standard across all IT groups.
- Define a procedure for database back-outs. Submit back-out scripts with all database change requests. Store and organize these scripts on a release server. This will eliminate reliance on e-mail request analysis and tape back-ups.
- Set service-level agreements (SLA) between database administrator (DBA) and the organization. An established cut-off point each day will allow for a more even flow of work for the DBAs.
- Set service-level agreements (SLA) between all organizations and their customers, both internal and external as well as with third-party vendors.
- Define procedures for impact analysis. Define contacts to perform the analysis as well as the appropriate stage for the analysis.
- Establish site standards for infrastructure configurations to facilitate site support and achieve economies of scale for equipment purchasing.
- Apply change management processes to all infrastructure changes.
- Define and document standard network component configuration management procedures.
- Design and document network testing procedures.
- Create a review process and checklist to verify proper implementation of network changes
- Develop a management procedure to gather, track, and refine project requirements.
- Formalize required documentation of all communications necessary to implement change.
- Establish a process for moving code from quality control into production, including signoffs and checklists.
- Develop and publish management procedures and responsibilities for infrastructure software (e.g., operating systems, monitoring software, etc.).

Technology

- Identify a central defect tracking system.
- Establish training for any new change management tools/processes implemented.

CONCLUSION

As depicted above, the deployment of an ERP system involves considerable business process analysis, employee retraining, and new work procedures. A production change management framework should plan, organize, lead, and control the activities needed to maintain the *legitimacy* of the ERP software programs. The framework should be a single management process dedicated to a common business focus. This order not only minimizes the effects of risk on an organization's ERP infrastructure but also minimizes financial, strategic, and operational risks.

In recent years, organizations have become more interested in ERP. Industry and government regulatory bodies, as well as investors, have begun to scrutinize companies' ERP risk-management policies and procedures. Ultimately, their success depends on striking a balance between enhancing security and managing risk.

Example 4A

Process Framework for ERP System Group

Example 4.A   Implementation Model

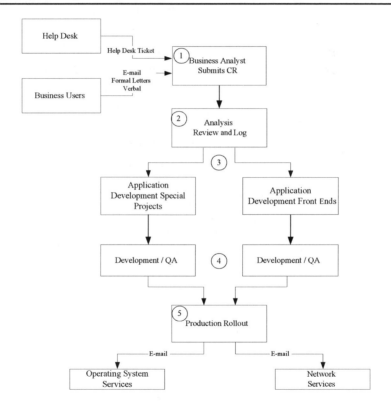

1. Change requests are communicated via help desk ticket, e-mail, formal letters, and verbally. The business analyst creates specifications, coordinates resources and assigns tasks to the developers.

2. The business analysts examine the business specifications. Spreadsheets are used by the analysts to track the status of changes to the system. The analysis process involves:
   - Determine defects or enhancements.
   - Identify severity and obtain customer approvals.
   - Use spreadsheets to track requests. Save e-mail requests.
   - Schedule weekly meetings to discuss projects.
   - Requirements document.
   - Assign project manager.
   - Define priorities.
   - Validate business analyst/customer.

3. The special projects and front-end development groups do their own development and quality assurance (QA).

4. Visual source safe is used for version control on the NT machines. There is no version control tool for the UNIX applications. There are separate QA servers. The development/QA process is as follows:

   Design → Development → Unit testing → Code review → User testing → QA testing → Production testing (on a test box)

Before moving into production, a preproduction form must be filled out, reviewed, and signed by a vice-president. This form includes developer job functions, general application information, and affected servers/environments. At production rollout time, e-mails are sent to operating system services and network services. Operating system services owns the production servers (see Example 4B).

Example 4B

Organizational Roles and Responsibilities for ERP Systems Engineering

Example 4B   Deployment Model

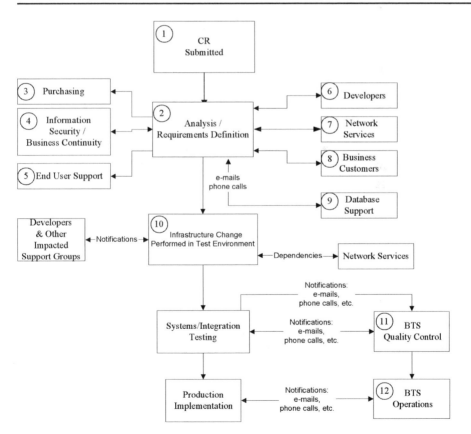

Systems Engineering is an ERP infrastructure support group that performs changes to the ERP system infrastructure: platform engineering, strategic services, project planning and management. It includes implementing and configuring network connectivity for the infrastructure that supports the ERP.

Process Framework for ERP Systems Engineering

1. Submit change requests via e-mail or phone calls. Infrastructure changes can be related to any ERP system.
2. Analyze change requests performed by systems engineering:
   - Address requirements and dependencies with developers, other support groups, and business representatives.
   - Exchange information through meetings and e-mails with attachments.
   - Complete a standard project initiation template and project definition template to record and validate scope and requirements related data.
   - Use a standard project ERP life cycle methodology and perform project planning/management.
   - Perform impact analysis and scheduling.
3. When hardware/software is purchased, submit a ticket to the ERP help desk that routes the request to the purchasing department.
4. Software engineering management determines if the information systems security group should be contacted. If so, communication is initiated via e-mail, meetings, etc. When the security group participates in a project, a project checklist is completed that includes highlights of security requirements and signoff fields for different stages of the change life cycle.
5. Contact the end user support group to manage physical space in the data center, installing racks and, occasionally, server components. Complete end user support request form.

6. Interface with developers to record and validate requirements, dependencies and impact analysis. Requirements recorded in a standard project definition report developed by software engineering.

7. Software engineering management determines if the change requires communication with network services. Network services utilizes a standard template called the *network services project description* to record network change requirements and a standard notification form called the *network change notice form* to log the change and for impact analysis, and so forth.

8. Software engineering communicates with business customers via project meetings, e-mails, and phone calls to review and validate some of the requirements.

9. Database requirements are obtained and may be included in the project definition template.

10. Infrastructure changes are performed in a test environment by software engineering. Other dependent groups external to software engineering participate in integration testing when needed. This may result in notifications (e-mails, phone calls, or meetings) to other potentially impacted support groups (e.g., network services).

11. ERP quality control group participates when integration of applications with hardware is tested for load, stress, capacity, function, and defining logical and physical directories.

12. ERP operations migrates application code to production and provides day-to-day operational support for the infrastructure that software engineering has implemented. Software engineering communicates infrastructure specifications (i.e., servers) and addresses technical issues (server configuration, fails, etc.) when necessary.

Technology for ERP Systems Engineering

UNIX, Windows NT, Oracle, Tivoli, SMS for server changes

Example 4C

Organizational Roles and Responsibilities for Data Management

The ERP Data Management group applies changes to databases, monitors performance of databases and plans the deployment and configuration of new databases.

Process Framework for ERP Data Management

1. Vendors send notification of changes (e.g., database software updates, data feeds, etc.) and updates to network services. Network services evaluates the merit of the change and sends change requests when appropriate.
2. Trusted vendors and third-party software are granted a direct path to production database change testing.
3. Change requests are submitted via e-mail with attachments.
4. Analysis of change requests performed by ERP data management. Information service, ERP systems engineering and information systems security and business continuity are contacted, as appropriate, for each change request. Requirements are defined and validated.
5. Tests of development database changes performed by ERP data management. If the testing of the change fails, an e-mail notification is sent back to the requestor. If the testing of the database change is successful, then that change is applied to the development environment and notification is sent to the developers.

Example 4C ERP Data Management Model

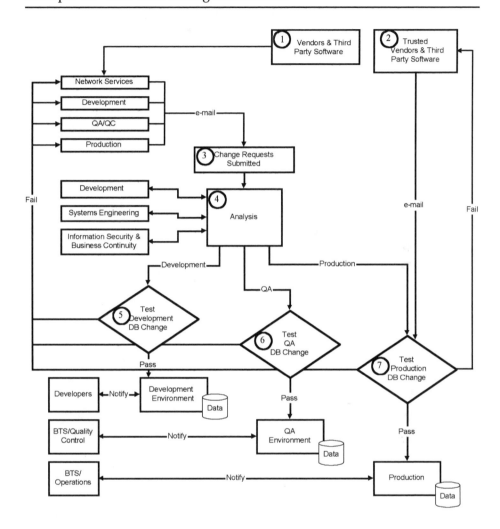

6. Tests of QA database changes performed by ERP data management. If the testing of the change fails, an e-mail notification is sent back to the requestor. If the testing of the database change is successful, that change is applied to the QA environment and notification is sent to ERP/QC.

7. Tests of production database changes performed by ERP data management. If the testing of the change fails, an e-mail

notification is sent back to the requestor. If the testing of the database change is successful, that change is applied to the production environment and notification is sent to the requestor and ERP/Operations.

Technology for ERP Data Management

UNIX, NT, Oracle, Sybase, SQL, Db Artisan

Example 4D

Organizational Roles and Responsibilities for ERP Production System

The production support group provides day-to-day operational support to the ERP System, marketing data services and their UNIX and NT servers.

Exhibit 4D   ERP Production Support Group Model

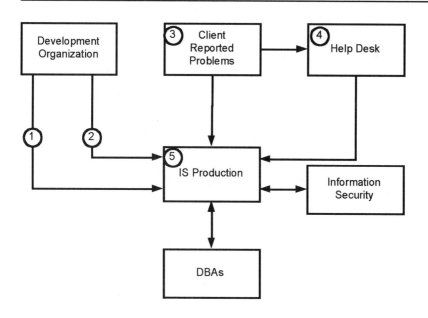

Process Framework for ERP Production Group

1. Information systems security production receives two types of requests from development organizations. There are promotion requests to move development changes into production. A *promotion request form* accompanies all of these promotion requests. However, ERP production is rarely informed of the full impact of the changes. The development area moves the changes to a special directory on the server. ERP production moves the changes into production.

2. Development requests data feeds from ERP production for transmission to outside vendors. ERP production does the scripting for these feeds. ERP production coordinates testing with the affected vendors. ERP production also handles setting up data feeds coming into the organization from outside vendors.

3. ERP production is the operations group for all batch processing on the UNIX System. Clients of the systems may report problems (missing reports, incorrect data values, etc.). Clients will either contact ERP production directly or contact the help desk with the problem.

4. Client-reported problems are sometimes reported to the help desk and then routed to ERP production. Client-reported problems can also be directly called into ERP production.

5. When appropriate, ERP production will contact information systems security regarding development requests. They also work with the DBAs when database changes are involved. The developer has to notify them of changes and coordinate the effort. ERP production runs their own applications to scan logs for job status. They also initiate their own projects for maintenance and trouble-shooting.

Technology for ERP Production Group

RJE (remote job entry) and SNA (system network architecture) protocols are used to connect to real-time gateway and to UNIX enterprise servers.

5

Post-implementation Issues and Controls

INTRODUCTION

The primary intention of this chapter is to provide audit with an understanding of the post-implementation concerns and controls in an ERP processing system. Rapid developments in ERP technology, along with significant expansion in the use of ERP systems for business in general, have increased the need for in-depth knowledge of ERP systems and related IT control procedures, as shown in Exhibit 5.1, ERP System Activities, and Exhibit 5.2, Responsibility Map.

This chapter is organized around a series of control questions. For ease of reference, related control questions are grouped together and each group is assigned a reference letter. A complete list of the control questions is included in Appendix 5A. In sections pertaining to application controls, general controls, and additional controls for advanced ERP systems, each question is discussed in detail under the following headings:

- *Background.* This discussion will provide an overview of the control procedures and will include illustrative examples and definitions of specialized terms.

- *Control procedures.* Many of the control procedures prescribed will be discussed under this heading.

Exhibit 5.1

ERP SYSTEM ACTIVITIES

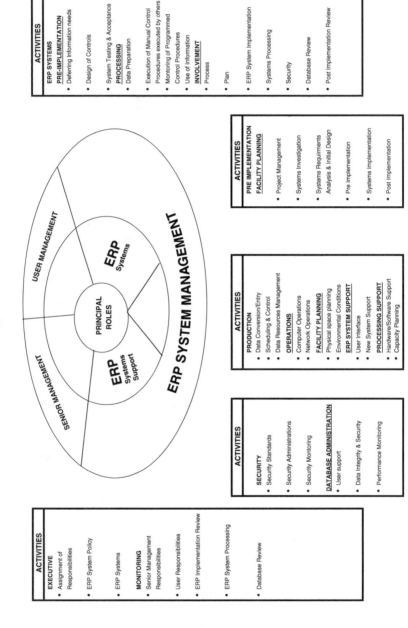

ACTIVITIES

ERP SYSTEMS

PRE-IMPLEMENTATION
- Deferring Information needs
- Design of Controls
- System Testing & Acceptance

PROCESSING
- Data Preparation
- Execution of Manual Control
- Procedures executed by others
- Monitoring of Programmed Control Procedures
- Use of Information

INVOLVEMENT
- Process
- Plan
- ERP System Implementation
- Systems Processing
- Security
- Database Review
- Post Implementation Review

ACTIVITIES

PRE IMPLEMENTATION
FACILITY PLANNING
- Project Management
- Systems Investigation
- Systems Requirments Analysis & Initial Design
- Pre Implementation
- Systems Implementation
- Post Implementation

ACTIVITIES

PRODUCTION
- Data Conversion/Entry
- Scheduling & Control
- Data Resources Management

OPERATIONS
- Computer Operations
- Network Operations

FACILITY PLANNING
- Physical space planning
- Environmental Conditions

ERP SYSTEM SUPPORT
- User Interface
- New System Support

PROCESSING SUPPORT
- Hardware/Software Support
- Capacity Planning

ACTIVITIES

SECURITY
- Security Standards
- Security Administrations
- Security Monitoring

DATABASE ADMINISTRATION
- User support
- Data Integrity & Security
- Performance Monitoring

ACTIVITIES

EXECUTIVE
- Assignment of Responsibilities
- ERP System Policy
- ERP Systems

MONITORING
- Senior Management Responsibilities
- User Responsibilities
- ERP Implementation Review
- ERP System Processing
- Database Review

154

Exhibit 5.2   Responsibility Map

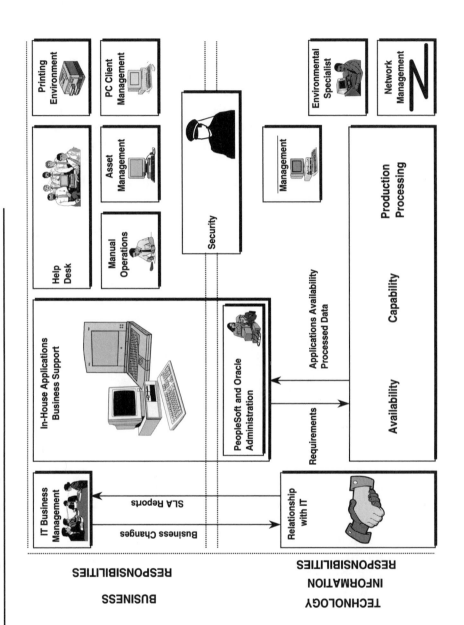

- *Minicomputers.*   The use of minicomputers has increased rapidly; their use has introduced additional control problems. Where relevant, discussion will describe control procedures in a minicomputer environment.
- *Compensating controls and significance of weaknesses.* Compensating controls are procedures established for another purpose but which provide a degree of compensation for a weakness with respect to the control being considered. The significance of control weaknesses to management and to audit will also be discussed under this heading.
- *Possible compliance tests.*   The compliance tests listed under each question will be viewed as a catalog for selecting or designing relevant tests.

In addition to our primary audit responsibilities, we should be alert to other audit service possibilities to provide advice on the effective design of control procedures. Significant weaknesses that come up during the course of the audit should be communicated to the ERP/IT group.

The information in this guide is designed to assist in providing effective post-implementation auditing services. It will help ERP system users process all kinds of business data more effectively and efficiently.

POST-IMPLEMENTATION PROBLEMS

Problems associated with ERP Implementations become more rampant during the post-implementation phase. Once users learn their way around the system, they test its limits, setting off shock waves that devastate an otherwise successful control environment. While extensive integration and acceptance testing will have flushed programming errors and exercised the various pathways through the system, post-implementation brings an explosion of bug reports along with a slew of frenzied requests for new functions. The post-implementation phase requires an ongoing process of improvement and fine-tuning. It is the greatest challenge to audit because audit is expected to unravel the root of problems in the ERP processes and provide effective solutions.

Post-implementation reviews reveal the unique learning curve that occurs for experienced users after the implementation of an ERP system. This learning curve is very different from the way clerical workers learn routine tasks. It often takes many months for experienced users to get comfortable with the system because, early in a system's life, these users tend to resist using it for their important work. Because they already have a set process and comfort level in getting their work done, the complex ERP systems may appear threatening and intrusive.

Many experienced users (at all levels of seniority) secretly harbor a fear of appearing stupid by failing to master such a tool. In response to these fears, many experienced users will greet the new system's implementation by continuing to do things as they always have. They will log on to the system occasionally to demonstrate to management that they are giving it a try. They will usually use those features of the system that require the least effort to learn and that pose the least risk of things going wrong. If the system includes a monitoring function that reports statistically on which functions of the system are being used, how often, and by whom (i.e., monitoring post-implementation), these patterns will be evident. It is often found that some users only use the system to receive mail and to look at calendars created by their secretaries; not to use the document creation routines themselves or to store files in the document database. They may also often override sophisticated automatic processing and only use manual functions that give them a greater feeling of control. They may prefer looking at reports to using online inquiry. It takes a period of months for users to begin to feel comfortable with their new tools. However, at some point in the ERP system's life history, as users begin to see the advantages of the new system, they gingerly begin to explore its functions, gradually getting over their shyness as their efforts are greeted with success. After all, the system would not have been implemented in the first place if it were not a terrific aid. Finally, as the post-implementation period sets in, a critical mass of users emerges, users who are enthusiastic about the system. And, most important, these users are beginning to understand, from a functional standpoint, how it operates.

At this point, an explosion takes place. Monitoring programs, if they are in place, will suddenly show a tremendous upsurge in the use of the system by all users. If the system includes communications features like electronic mail or work group computing, enough people in the user group are sufficiently comfortable with such features to begin to use them instead of the telephone or paper documents. If the system tracks investment or accounts, the users may start relying on online inquiry in place of hardcopy reports, and use all the sophisticated transactions that have been provided.

Finally, having mastered the system, the users begin to get creative. Now they are likely to apply their functional understanding of how the system appears to operate and try to push it a step further than it was designed to go. They will start using the system to deal with (or attempt to deal with) situations that were not envisioned by the system's designers, no matter how hard the designers tried to imagine the system in operation.

It is at this point, when a critical mass of users is fully using the system, bringing to it all their ingenuity and creativity, that post-implementation aftershock strikes and the bug reports start flooding the maintenance group. The bugs reported are rarely trivial and are difficult to track down. Many of these bugs result from users doing tricky things with the system in hopes of *faking it out*. For example, some users will understand how a parameter file controls what can be done with the system. And, they start to alter parameters temporarily to slip in transactions that contain combinations of field values needed in a particular case not anticipated by the system's designers. Without such finagling, the transactions would not make it through a series of online edits; but with the finagling, they would. Having made their changes, the users then politely change the parameter file back to its earlier values. These tricks generate records that cause problems in the subsystem. It takes major detective work to determine the source of these illegal records.

At the same time these bugs are occurring, requests pour in from the same users for more function. The functions requested are often complex, and user management may start wondering why such an *obvious* function was not included in the original systems design.

This slew of system requests is not a sign of bad design; rather, it is a sign of the system's success! It shows that the users have accepted the system and are putting it to use. It also demonstrates that the experienced users are confident enough to go beyond a cookbook approach to using the system and are becoming creative and innovative partners in the system's design. Now, having digested the system that they wanted, these sophisticated users want to push the system's limits further. It is highly unrealistic to expect representatives of system groups or user groups to be able to design into the initial version of a complex ERP system every feature that experienced users would require. That is why commercial ERP systems are developed in a series of releases.

Why Aftershock Can Devastate

The complex and challenging requirements posed by the ERP system's newly sophisticated users emerge just when there is no one left on the project with a good grasp of the project's existing design; and the analysis and debugging skills needed to meet the user's new needs. Management, lulled by the system's initial months of quiet and certain that excellent ERP implementation methodology has finally paid off; tend to strip projects of capable resources, sending them on to hot new projects. Thus, the users do not get the changes they need at the time they are most excited about using the system. Or worse, they may get changes that do not work properly or that "break" other previously working parts of the system. Unfortunately, this can set the stage for an ongoing adversarial relationship between the users and the ERP systems department. In the worst cases, managers involved in the ERP system's implementation get blamed for producing a system that has become an embarrassment to the systems area.

How can you best prepare for post-implementation aftershock? There is no way to avoid aftershock in the project's post-implementation phase. It is a maintenance phase phenomenon and should be treated as such. The position that maintenance can be omitted or bypassed by "correct" implementation is not only unrealistic; it fails to give the maintenance phase of a project the respect it deserves. Aftershock cannot be eliminated during the testing phase; unless the test phase is expanded to include the acquisition of a critical of mass of experienced users. In the test phase, those doing the testing are either those who developed the specifications for the system (who are too familiar with how the system is expected to operate to truly stress it in new and ingenious ways) or they are the "real users" who have not yet shifted gears from their current non-system-oriented methods to methods in which the ERP system is an integral part of their jobs. Only the emergence of a critical mass of users creates the stress that can result in post-implementation aftershock. By monitoring the system usage, you can determine when that critical mass has formed and whether the system can withstand its pressure.

It is vital to expect aftershock and to budget for it. Ideally, project management will consider this phase a part of final testing and budget accordingly. It is essential to retain the services of the people who implemented the system; since it is at this stage that the users request the most useful and, to them, necessary, enhancements to the system. If the project depends heavily on outside consultants for programming support, plan to use the heavy consultant support for this phase; not just for the three months after implementation.

Prepare User Management

Prepare user management for the advent of this phase and make sure that they understand that its emergence is a sign of the system's success and proof that the users are really using it. Make sure that they save some of their implementation budget for the resources they will need to participate in this final fine-tuning of the system's design.

Don't abandon methodology just because implementation is over. Most implementation groups now operate under the influence of some kind of ERP implementation methodology. Most require some kind of design review and usually demand that documentation be produced along with system design. Unfortunately, since the aftershock occurs when implementation is over and maintenance has begun; methodology has often become a thing of the past, replaced by a bug-oriented change control system that controls code fixes at a module inspection level.

This means that the system enhancements made as a result of post-implementation aftershock all too often are made without the benefits of ERP methodology. These enhancements are often treated as independent code fixes rather than as a return to the system analysis and design phase. Usually, these enhancements are not made one at a time; but are proposed and added to the system at the same time as a whole constellation. Unless they are managed as a unit, using strict ERPLC methodology; disaster is assured. Since many of these user-originated new features are highly sophisticated and very important to the system's ongoing integrity; it is vital that they work. They must be developed, coded, and tested with the same rigor as was the original system. Otherwise they will fail, spectacularly, in a manner that will give the entire ERP system team a black eye.

Finally, during the frenzy of system testing, many implementation managers tend to postpone adding the many small changes that the users' representatives come up with during the latter part of the implementation process. Rather than risk falling behind on tight implementation schedules by attempting to add them to the system during testing; they postpone these design change requests for 6 to 12 months after implementation. They think that after six months the system will have become *stable* and these expected changes can be quietly slipped in. Nothing could be further from the truth. It would be better to put expected changes in right after implementation during the "quiet period" that occurs before the users really take to the system, or else to wait until the aftershock has occurred. Implementing the new code required by these many small changes, simultaneously with those for the enhancements to satisfy newly sophisticated users, can quickly destabilize the most stable system. The many months of hectic debugging that can ensue can give what may have been a good ERP system a bad reputation from which it may never recover.

Monitoring Aftershock

If the thought of post-implementation aftershock makes you quake, take heart. There is a way to prepare and protect the project from disaster by measuring stress on a system. The best way to track aftershock is to design a function into the new ERP system that monitors system usage in terms of transactions or function used and how often, breaking that usage down by individuals. See Exhibit 5.3 for a post-implementation monitoring aftershock model. This information is usually available in the system already, but not presented in an accessible report format. This function should generate reports that go to project management on a weekly basis during the first months of the system's life. It is often a good idea to have a version of this information go to the user group management. These reports will give information that is helpful in several respects.

By identifying shy users, the ERP system makes it possible to give extra help to those individuals who most need it, early in the ERP system's life history, thus accelerating the learning curve for the group. Ideally, those responsible for training users can send someone to drop by users' desks casually and give inconspicuous help to those who need it most, without singling them out as deficient.

Such monitoring may show that whole sections of the new ERP system are not being used. These areas are where you can expect a lot of aftershock activity. For example, if the new system is being phased in and only being used for new customer accounts until some older system is converted, you may find that a whole subset of transactions appropriate for older accounts is never being used. These transactions are the ones most likely to show up on bug reports a year down the line when the new accounts have matured. It is important to track this because often, the conversion of older systems, along with the enhancements of the new implemented ERP systems, is scheduled for six months to a

162

Exhibit 5.3   Post-implementation—Monitoring Aftershock Model

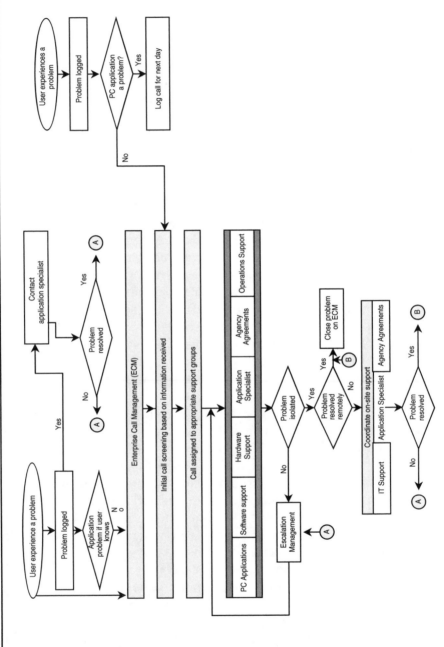

year after implementation, when the ERP system is expected to be stable. By avoiding mixing conversions with aftershock, both phases of the project can be completed with a minimum of confusion.

ERP CONTROLS AND THE AUDIT PROCESS

Planning and Staffing

Responsibility for the planning and execution of an audit of internal controls of clients using computer systems rests with the audit staff, headed by the engagement partner and manager. In many situations, the review of the IT aspects of internal control may be performed by both the operations and IT audit staff working jointly. Under some circumstances, the audit may have to be performed by the IT auditors because of the specialized skills required. However, during the engagement, there is no reason why the IT and operations auditors cannot communicate effectively. This discussion has been developed to facilitate communications between the operations and IT auditors.

The IT auditors should function as integral members of the audit team. The IT auditors participation could include consultation in the development of the audit plan, specified reviews of general and application controls, and development of computer assisted auditing techniques (CAAT). The application of specialized knowledge and experience should be integrated into the audit process under the direction of the audit manager. The evaluation and testing of IT controls should not be treated as a separate activity.

Updating the Information Base

The control review begins during the first phase of the ERPLC. Information gathered during this phase should give a broad overview of the financial and business systems and related controls, as well as enabling preparation of the audit plan. In a recurring audit engagement, it is important to focus on the system changes since the preceding audit. This overview should normally comprise:

- An awareness of the manual, mechanical, and ERP methods used for each significant financial and business application in use.

- An appreciation of the characteristics of significant ERP systems; for example, whether they are batch-controlled, online, or integrated, and whether they use databases, distributed data processing, or minicomputers.
- An understanding of the flow of transactions through both the manual and ERP portions of each significant financial and business system.
- An awareness of the structure of accounting, financial and operational controls; including the relative reliance on user controls and ERP processing controls; and the importance of general controls to each significant individual application system.

Documentation of the control review results is an important part of the information base. Systems documentation in the audit files should enable us to prepare an effective and efficient audit plan. Present and future audit teams using the files should be able to understand the audit significance of the systems and control procedures.

For some systems, a narrative description may be sufficient to document how the system operates. For other systems, it may be more effective to record parts or all of the system in the form of flowcharts supplemented by narrative notes. Frequently, it may be possible to use the ERP systems documentation as a basis for audit files.

Audit Approach

The audit approach should be planned to achieve specific objectives. The potential sources of evidence available should be identified. How our examination of this evidence will satisfy our objectives should be evaluated. Audit procedures, which can be used to examine the evidence, should be determined.

Sufficient and substantive tests of evidence supporting significant transactions and balances will satisfy our objectives. Considering the extent of reliance on the accuracy of the client's financial and business systems, and the effectiveness of their internal controls, is an important strategic decision in planning. A "systems based approach" will stress compliance tests of the client's control procedures. This permits reducing the scope or altering the nature of our substantive tests of evidence.

ERP systems are often used in significant financial and business applications which process large volumes of data. In these circumstances, it is usually more efficient and effective to adopt a systems-based approach. However, it may be more efficient and effective to obtain the entire audit evidence from substantive tests. The use of computer-assisted auditing techniques can enable more efficient selection, testing, and analysis of evidence and reduction of reliance on the testing of internal control procedures.

Identification and Testing of Key Controls

The review, evaluation, and testing of ERP controls is not an end in itself. The control procedures listed in this chapter should not be regarded as equally important. Rather, an attempt to identify the small number of key controls should be made. A key control must fulfill two conditions:

1. It must be a control procedure which, provided it is functioning effectively, will contribute significantly toward ensuring that the financial and business system produces reliable information.

2. It must be a control procedure relied upon to evaluate the control framework.

The phrase *auditing around the computer* is used to describe an audit approach that traces source documents to computer output reports without regard to the details of ERP processing. In many circumstances, this can be an appropriate approach. However, ERP controls should not be ignored when auditing around the computer. Reliance on user controls is needed to ensure that the client's records are complete.

In identifying key controls, user controls (or other application controls) should be considered first. Those specific control procedures that are most efficient and effective should be selected. Certain general controls are essential for complete and accurate processing (for example, controls to prevent unauthorized changes to production files (files containing original information about the clients business activities) in the ERP system.

The audit plan should include audit tests designed to obtain evidence that the key control procedures are operating effectively.

Minicomputers

With the increased use of relatively small, inexpensive computers for complex applications, the distinction between large computers (mainframes) and minicomputers is becoming less clear. The following important elements generally characterize a minicomputer installation.

- *Staffing.* A minicomputer is normally operated by a relatively small number of staff who are part of the user department.
- *Location.* A minicomputer is often located within the user department with little or no control over physical access.
- *Programs.* Many minicomputer installations use application systems supplied by software vendors or equipment manufacturers. In cases where the user writes programs, there is an increasing use of *easy-to-learn* programming languages that facilitate program development.
- *Processing mode.* The systems often use online data entry and file updating.

The term *microcomputer* is sometimes used to refer to very small computers. In this guide, the term *minicomputers* includes microcomputers, LANs and WANs.

General controls may not be as sophisticated or reliable in a minicomputer environment as in a large computer environment. Consequently, reliance on user controls may increase. Control problems in an ERP installation often include:

- *Lack of segregation of duties.* Large computer installations usually have separate groups of staff within the IT department for programming, operations, and control of data. In a minicomputer installation, one or two people often perform the functions of systems analysis, system design, programming, maintenance of software, and operations. They may also be responsible for controlling data files and entering transactions.
- *Inadequate software processing controls.* Minicomputer application systems are often purchased from manufacturers or software vendors that do not offer desirable online control techniques. Vendors and users may believe that the expense of developing adequate controls and the additional processing costs are not warranted.

- *Ready access to data files and programs.* In many minicomputer installations, current versions of master files and programs are always available for online inquiries and updating.
- *Inadequate file and program backup procedures.* Many companies that use minicomputers have all operating and administrative functions located in a single building with no offsite storage facilities readily available. A fireproof safe or filing cabinet may be considered an unnecessary expense. User personnel may not create backup files because they do not understand the need or because of the length of time needed to create copy files.

CLASSIFICATION OF ERP CONTROL PROCEDURES

Auditing literature is not consistent in its definition of categories of control procedures. In this discussion, ERP controls will be divided between those that relate to a specific system (application controls) and those that relate to the overall information technology function (general controls). A number of controls (over program changes, backup procedures, and so forth.) that are considered general controls in traditional batch systems are often application-related in contemporary systems, particularly in online systems and where minicomputers are used for single ERP applications.

Application Controls

User Controls over Transactions

> *Are there user controls over the preparation and approval of transactions?*

It is important to ensure users properly approve the transactions before they are submitted for processing.

Background

Approval of input data is the first stage of user control over data for ERP processing. Approval or authorization of input, outside the ERP system function, is an important aspect of the segregation of duties between users and ERP system staff.

In sophisticated ERP systems, the programs often perform some authorization procedures, such as the checking of customer orders for credit status and inventory availability. In such a system, an accepted order may lead to the generation of shipping documents by the ERP system, which will serve as authority for the release of goods from a warehouse.

Control Procedures

- Use of standard, numerically sequenced input forms, controlled by the users.
- Authorization of significant input transactions by user department management.

Compensating Controls and Significance of Weaknesses

Some errors in input may be detected automatically by validation or edit checks carried out by the ERP system. However, these checks cannot be relied upon to identify all errors. For example, an edit check on pricing might reveal the incorrect pricing of an inventory issue but would not identify a totally fictitious issue, entered at the correct price for that category of item.

Possible Compliance Tests

- Test procedures for maintaining numerical control over input documents.
- Review a selection of processed input documents for proper approval in the user department.
- Trace a sample of input documents into the batch controls.

Control over Input

Does the user control input?

It is important to ensure that all input approved by the user is processed through the system in the correct accounting period and that each transaction is not processed more than once.

Background

Control over the input of transaction data should be established as close to its source as possible. Generally, the user department should take the final responsibility for ensuring that all approved input is properly processed.

Control Procedures

- Use of prenumbered source documents. The user department should keep a record of documents used and ensure that these are subsequently processed. Missing documents should be accounted for to ensure that only authorized transactions are processed and to identify transactions not processed.
- Batching procedures. These may be used to control the number of documents entered and the total monetary or numerical amount of critical fields within batches. This helps assure that the transactions submitted are accurately entered and processed through the system. Batching procedures may include:
  - Preparation of batch or hash totals on critical fields. Hash totals are control totals established by adding together numerical fields within batches of documents. Although meaningless in themselves, these totals can help identify errors and omissions. The arithmetic total of the account numbers used in a batch of journal entries is an example. If one or more of the account numbers is entered incorrectly, the total of the account numbers entered will not agree with the hash total.
  - Preparation and approval of batch header and transmittal control forms, including control totals for balancing purposes. The approval of these forms by user management helps provide assurance that batching procedures are properly applied.

- ◦ Numerical control over batches that helps detect unauthorized batches and identify missing batches.

- ◦ A control log for recording batch information. This log should be maintained by the user department to facilitate follow-up on batches submitted for processing and to detect modifications made to batches after they have left the user department. Procedures to ensure that the final batch of each accounting period is processed are particularly important.

- ◦ Reconciliation by user staff of input totals to output totals to establish that no data has been lost or added during processing and to help ensure the accuracy of data entry and processing. The individual responsible for the reconciliation should not have incompatible responsibilities such as data conversion.

- ◦ Recording by users of the number of batches that contain errors and the nature of those errors. This record is valuable since frequent or recurring errors may indicate that proper procedures are not being followed.

- ◦ Control totals on individual input documents. If input is not batched, each document should carry value or hash totals of significant fields to help ensure accurate entry.

- ◦ One-for-one manual checks from computer listings to input documents, and vice versa. This is generally a very inefficient alternative to batch controls.

Compensating Controls and Significance of Weaknesses

Compensating controls may include:

- • A data control group responsible for the batch controls and reconciliation procedures. Where there are several users, a central control group apart from the user departments may enforce some of these controls. Each user submits input documents to the control group, which compiles appropriate batch controls, before the documents are sent to the ERP department. There should be an adequate review of output by both the control group and each user.
- • Extensive data validation and completeness checks by computer programs.
- • Detailed scrutiny of output by users.

If there are no compensating controls, audit may need to increase the scope of audit procedures to obtain evidence on the completeness and accuracy of processing.

Possible Compliance Tests

Select batches from the batch control log or from the actual batches processed through the system during the period to:

- Test numerical sequence.
- Check correct dating.
- Check the batch totals for document count, value totals, and hash totals.
- Check user's approval of the batch header and transmittal control forms.
- Trace the batches to the batch control log.
- Test the totals on the batch control log.
- Trace batch totals to the edit program or other intermediate program printout.
- Scan the input control records to confirm that they have been properly prepared and to identify unprocessed batches.
- Review and test client's reconciliations of input totals to output totals. Check that these reconciliation have been approved by management.
- Review client's record of batches that contain errors.
- If input is not batched, test controls over individual input documents, one-for-one checking, and so forth.

User Controls over Standing Data

Are there user controls over changes to standing data on master files, look-up tables and databases?

It is important to ensure that all changes to standing data are authorized and completely and accurately processed.

Background

A master file usually contains both cumulative transaction data and standing data. Controls over cumulative transaction data are discussed later on in the chapter. Standing data is information that changes relatively rarely and that may be used during each processing cycle. It comprises general reference data (e.g., names and addresses, reference codes, categories, and status codes) and accounting values (e.g., rates of pay, interest, depreciation or discount, and inventory unit costs). Often, when standing data is common to several categories of items (e.g., employees, customers, suppliers, inventory items, or fixed assets), it will be held in separate data files or *look-up tables* or incorporated in the program coding. The master files will often not contain the full standing data, but *indicators* that will direct the computer programs to the appropriate look-up table or coding.

Changes to standing data may comprise insertion of records, changes to records, and deletion of records. In some systems obsolete records are deleted automatically by *weeding* programs. Such obsolete records might include dormant customers or suppliers, obsolete inventory items, or former employees. Once a change is made to standing data, it will affect all subsequent processing until it is changed again. *Therefore, the completeness and accuracy of standing data should be carefully controlled. The users should impose this control.*

Some systems allow certain standing data, such as sales prices, discount rates, or interest rates, to be overridden for an individual transaction by the input of additional data at the same time as the transaction itself. *Override instructions should be controlled as tightly as other changes to standing data.*

Control Procedures

- Use of specifically designed forms and input screens for the inputting changes to help prevent errors in preparation.
- Use of prenumbered input forms, restricted to and controlled by authorized personnel.
- Initiation or approval of input forms for changes by user department management.
- Establishment of batch control totals of changes by the user and subsequent reconciliation with a printout of changes. This

control is only appropriate if the volume of changes is relatively large.

- A printout detailing all the changes processed. A manager not immediately involved in the preparation of the changes should review this. In some large organizations, a central control function rather than the originating user department may review the printout. The extent to which the changes from the printout to authorized source documents should be checked will depend upon the volume of changes processed and the importance of the standing data changed.
- Individual authorization of all override instructions.
- Computer listing of all override instructions for review by management.

Compensating Controls and Significance of Weaknesses

It is difficult to compensate for weaknesses in user controls over changes to standing data. The following procedures may, however, reduce the risk associated with weak user controls:

- Adequate control over the continuing completeness and accuracy of standing data.
- Programmed validity and reasonableness checks on changes. Such controls may, for example, check that account code numbers are valid; that basic pay is not in excess of a specified amount, or that duplicate records are not created.

Even when a central ERP data control group performs these procedures, the user should still review the output for reasonableness, as an additional check that unauthorized changes have not been processed.

Possible Compliance Tests

- Test numerical control procedures over input forms.
- Select printouts of master file and database changes and:
  - Check the user's reconciliation of control totals to the printouts.

- ○ Inspect the source documents authorizing the changes.
- ○ Check proper authorization of the source documents.
- ○ Select source documents and trace to the printout of changes.
- Select printouts of rejected changes and:
  - ○ Determine that the report contains sufficient detail for the user to correct errors.
  - ○ Check that the items have been rejected for valid reasons.
  - ○ Check that all errors were corrected and resubmitted promptly.
- Trace errors to the correcting entries and to evidence of correct changes on the master file and databases.
- Check proper authorization of corrected entries.
- Select printouts of override instructions and:
  - ○ Inspect source documents.
  - ○ Check that source documents are properly authorized.
  - ○ Inspect evidence of management review and approval of printout.

Are there user controls over the continuing completeness and accuracy of standing data on master files, databases, and look-up tables?

It is important to ensure the continuing completeness and accuracy of data that may be used during each processing cycle.

Background

Controls over a user's changes to standing data will not necessarily detect unauthorized changes made by:

- Another user with access to the master file.
- A central data control function.
- ERP personnel.

Therefore the procedures described in question B1 should be supplemented by further procedures to verify the continuing completeness and accuracy of the standing data.

Control Procedures

- Reconciling user control totals with computer-accumulated totals of the number of records maintained on file, and of significant standing data fields.
- Verifying the continuing completeness and accuracy of standing data in individual records. This may involve periodic full listings, cyclical sampling, or ad hoc inquiries on specified records for checking with user records.

Compensating Controls and Significance of Weaknesses

The client's computer installation may include software facilities that prevent unauthorized changes to standing data. Weaknesses in this area may have a major effect on the degree of reliance that may be placed on accounting records produced using the standing data.

Possible Compliance Tests

- Review and test check the client's reconciliation of standing data totals reported by the computer with manual records.
- Check the existence of printouts indicating that the standing data totals for individual master records have been accumulated and reconciled to control records by the computer system.
- Check that standing data has been periodically printed and checked in accordance with the client's procedures; for example, by use of inquiry or sampling programs.
- Test the accuracy of standing data to and from the client's printouts; if these are not available, use special printouts produced for audit purposes.

User Controls over Rejections and Suspense Items

Are there user controls over rejected transactions?

Purpose of the Controls

The purpose of controls is to ensure that all rejected items are promptly corrected and processed, with particular regard to proper accounting cut-off.

Background

A transaction may fail an edit check if, for example, the account number is missing or the check digit of the account number is incorrect. Depending upon the design of the ERP system, invalid or unmatched input data may be:

- Accepted by the system and highlighted in an exception report.
- Directed into a suspense account within the system.
- Rejected entirely.

Rejected items, suspense items, and items accepted but reported as exceptions are discussed here.

Normally when data is rejected entirely, the ERP system does not retain any record of the item; consequently, the rejected data must be controlled manually. The user is generally responsible for ensuring that such transactions are subsequently corrected.

Control Procedures

- Maintenance of a manual register that records rejected items and their subsequent reprocessing. This register may comprise annotated copies of computer listings of rejections.
- Separate batching of corrected rejections. This procedure makes it easier to ensure that all rejections are dealt with.
- Correction of rejections due to source document errors by the originating user department and resubmission for processing under normal input controls, including authorization.
- Periodic analyses of rejections, by materiality, cause, aging, and cut off. This allows management to determine if rejections are caused by poor input procedures and to evaluate the impact of such errors.

- Entering of appropriate accounting cut-off adjustments at period ends for outstanding rejections.
- Manual processing of rejected data (e.g., the preparation of a manual sales invoice or payslip). This is an inefficient control but can be acceptable when rejection volumes are very low. In such cases, the computer data files should be promptly updated with properly authorized manual amounts.

Compensating Controls and Significance of Weaknesses

Compensating controls may include:

- Holding invalid items on an ERP suspense file.
- Controls exercised by the ERP data control function.
- Management procedures such as strict budgetary analysis or management review of output.
- Checking of the numerical sequence of input documents by the ERP system with reporting of any missing documents.

The fact that users do not maintain documentary evidence that rejected transactions are appropriately controlled does not necessarily mean that rejections are corrected and promptly resubmitted. Nonetheless, the biggest risk here is that users may be unaware that a transaction was rejected and, thus, not corrected.

Whether an apparent weakness is serious enough to warrant a change of audit scope can usually be determined. The types of transactions that could potentially remain uncorrected, and their volume, should be determined first. If the volume is low and the transactions are not of a material nature, the potential effect of the weaknesses may not warrant additional work. If the volume is high or the transactions could be material, it may be necessary to change or increase the scope of procedures to confirm that transactions have been recorded in the proper period and that no significant transactions have remained unprocessed.

Possible Compliance Tests

- Review analyses of rejected input for selected periods to confirm that appropriate management action has been taken.
- Obtain manual register or printout of rejected transactions and:

- ○ Check that the report contains sufficient detail for the user to correct errors.
- ○ Confirm that the items were rejected for valid reasons.
- ○ Confirm that all errors were corrected and resubmitted promptly.
- ○ Check that the user's manual control records were correctly adjusted.
- ○ Select corrected entries and trace them through the system, checking proper correction of the data files.
- ○ Confirm proper authorization of corrected entries.
- • Review and test check client's batching procedures for corrections to ensure that all rejections are corrected promptly.
- • Review and test check cut-off adjustments for unprocessed corrections.

Does the user control suspense items?

Purpose of the Controls

The purpose is to ensure that items held in suspense within the computer system are all resolved correctly and promptly, with particular emphasis on proper accounting cut off.

Background

As discussed above, invalid or unmatched data may, in some ERP systems, be accepted into the computer to be held on separate suspense files pending resolution. The main causes of suspense items are:

- • Invalid input detected by edit programs.
- • Failure of update programs to match transactions with master records, databases, and so forth.
- • Failure of update programs to allocate credits against outstanding debit transactions and vice versa. This commonly happens with unallocated cash in an accounts receivable system.

- Failure of master file, databases, and maintenance programs to match standing data changes with existing master records. This may result in the automatic creation of dummy records.

In practice, items are more commonly held in suspense because of update program mismatches than because of invalid input.

Suspense items may be held within the ERP system on one or more of the following bases:

- On separate physical suspense files.
- Within separate suspense records on master files.
- Among the other records on the master files, identified by indicators or markers as separate transaction types.

Using a suspense file to correct invalid or unmatched transactions generally creates less risk than using exception reports.

Resolution of suspense items may be affected automatically by the ERP system, following necessary amendments to standing data, or by adjustments entered by the user. In both cases the user must remain ultimately responsible for the correct processing of the data.

Control Procedures

- Subjection of documents used to allocate, transfer, or write off suspense items to the same controls as all other input documents. Such documents should be correctly authorized and checked by user department management.
- Reconciliation of the net movement in suspense items with file update reports for each processing cycle.
- Checking all adjustments initiated by users with authorized input documents.
- Manual testing of a sample of ERP-generated adjustments.
- Investigation of exceptional items reported by the system (e.g., old outstanding items and material amounts) to determine whether appropriate corrective action has been taken, especially regarding accounting cut off.

Compensating Controls and Significance of Weaknesses

Compensating controls may include IT management or internal audit reviews to ensure user follow-up of these items. If there are no controls in this area, suspense transactions may not be promptly processed against the proper records.

Possible Compliance Tests

- Review analyses of suspense items for selected periods to confirm that appropriate management action has been taken.
- Review and test client's reconciliations of the net movement in total suspense items with file update reports.
- Obtain the listing of suspense items and:
  - Confirm that the listing contains sufficient detail for the user to correct errors.
  - Confirm that the items were placed on suspense for valid reasons.
  - Confirm that suspense items were resolved promptly.
  - Select suspense adjustments and trace them through the system, confirming proper correction of the data files.
  - Check that all adjustments were properly authorized.
  - Check the user's reconciliation of outstanding items.
- Review and test check cut off adjustments for unprocessed corrections.
- Check that client's procedures for manual testing of ERP-generated adjustments are being followed.

User Controls over Output

> **Are there user controls over output?**

Purpose of the Controls

The purpose of the controls is to detect errors and irregularities in output.

Background

Application programs will usually include provisions for printing control totals at various processing stages, including each of the final output reports. Users should reconcile these totals with their manually developed control totals to ensure that all input data is correctly processed; and that cumulative data brought forward from the previous processing cycle is correctly updated. Program-to-program controls should also be in effect for each application so that the computer system itself checks that all input and generated data are processed completely through all stages. These reconciliation procedures should account for rejections, suspense items, and updates of more than one file. *Users responsible for reviewing and reconciling output should not have other responsibilities that would be incompatible with the control of output, such as data conversion.*

Additional controls are required when output is produced in the form of negotiable instruments or as authority to make payments. ERP systems are sometimes used to generate presigned checks, interest or dividend warrants, and so forth.

Generally, good input and output controls go together; weakness in one area can negate the effectiveness of the other.

Control Procedures

- Reconciliation of movement on the master record to control totals prepared manually by users. This ensures that the total cumulative data, including suspense items, carried forward from the previous cycle plus current input equals the total carried forward at the end of the current cycle.
- Reconciliation of ERP-generated output and intermediate control totals to input control totals. This ensures that all submitted data has been processed.
- Reconciliation of the total accepted input as summarized in the edit validation reports and any generated data reported by other programs to the file update report. This ensures that all accepted transactions have been processed.
- Reconciliation of the movement between two updates to the transactions entered or generated. This ensures that the correct

files have been processed, i.e., previous carried forward total equals current brought forward total (cycle-to-cycle checks).

- Checking of other ERP totals, such as:
  - Program-to-program (run-to-run) totals, where several programs are used in sequence to perform all necessary processing of data.
  - Related output totals—for example, accounts receivable, aged analysis, listing of accounts receivable, invoice register, and sales ledger update report.
- Procedures to restrict the distribution of confidential output reports to authorized persons.
- Use of numerically controlled negotiable documents that are held securely at all times.
- Management review of output documents prepared in the form of negotiable instruments. Instruments above a specified amount should be countersigned outside the IT department.
- Specification of retention periods for source documents, data files, COM (computer output to microfilm), and printed output. These periods should be adequate for purposes of the client's operations and satisfy any legal requirements. There should be proper filing and cross-referencing of source documents and computer output.
- Adequate procedures for specifying exception conditions and for dealing with exception reports, including reports of invalid or unmatched data accepted for processing. The user should ensure that exception-reporting criteria are realistic, beneficial, and up to date. Exception reports should be dated, annotated with the action taken, and filed.
- Review of printed output by user management to see that it is reasonable, thereby detecting obvious processing errors.

Compensating Controls and Significance of Weaknesses

This is one of the most important areas of computer-related control for any application system. If control by the user is not effective, then it should be determined if another group, such as an independent data control group, is exercising this control. If not, the need to increase the scope of audit procedures should be considered.

Possible Compliance Tests

- Review and test check the client's reconciliation of output totals to input and cumulative data totals.
- Test additions of final output and trace to the financial records.
- Select file updates and inspect evidence of user procedures for:
  - Tracing input control totals through run-to-run controls to file update reports.
  - Tracing generated data control totals through run-to-run controls to file update reports.
  - Reconciling totals that are brought forward on file update reports with the previous reports (cycle-to-cycle controls).
  - Reconciling computer file update to manual controls.
  - Confirming that the outstanding totals of suspense items are correctly included in the above reconciliation.
  - Reconciling totals on computer listings of balances, and so forth, with file update reports.
  - Reconciling totals on computer analyses and reports, e.g., accounts receivable aged analysis, with file update reports.
  - Reconciling related output totals where more than one data file is updated, e.g., outstanding items, master and history files.
- Confirm that the user has reviewed the output for reasonableness and that action is taken following queries.
- Check that procedures to restrict the distribution of confidential reports to authorized persons are effective.
- Confirm that negotiable documents that constitute output are signed or countersigned outside the IT department.
- Test controls over unused negotiable instruments.
- Check that the client's retention policies for output documents are observed.
- Select significant exception reports and check that:
  - The reports contain sufficient detail for the user to correct errors.
  - Items were printed out for valid reasons.
  - Appropriate action was taken promptly and properly authorized.

- Serial numbering or dates indicate that all reports produced have been retained.
- Material exception reports are produced regularly.
- Items not fully dealt with appear on the subsequent reports.
- Select a sample of generated transactions from printouts and:
  - Check standing data with user records, such as personnel records and price lists.
  - Check posting to printout of ledger accounts.
  - Check calculations and additions.
  - Scan the printouts and obtain satisfactory explanations from users for large or unusual items.
  - Compare totals with user records.

ERP Processing Controls over Input

> *Are there controls over key transcription?*

Purpose of the Controls

The purpose is to ensure that data is key transcribed completely and accurately from input documents into a form that can be read by a computer.

Background

Key transcription is the process of transferring data from manually prepared input documents into computer-readable form. It may be performed using keypunch machines, key-to-disk (or key-to-tape) encoders, monitor screens, or various other facilities.

In a conventional batch-processing system, input data is batched by the users and sent to the ERP department for processing. At the ERP department, the batches will normally be received and recorded by an ERP control section prior to going to the key transcription section. In some systems, however, key transcription may be performed within user departments and only the encoded data sent to the ERP department.

Control Procedures

- Written instructions prescribing key transcription requirements for each type of input transaction.
- Written instructions including sample copies of all source documents used.
- Requirements for important input fields to be key verified. Rekeying the data to check the accuracy of the initial key transcription performs key verification. If there are any differences between the rekeying and the initial keying, the entry is rejected and must be re-entered. It is possible for employees to bypass key verification procedures. This risk can best be limited by adequate supervision.
- Marking or canceling of source documents to prevent duplicate processing.
- Recording of source documents received.
- Supervision of key transcription work.
- Restriction of access to source documents.
- Uses of key-to-disk batch balancing. Under this procedure batch control data is key transcribed along with the individual data items. The machine then adds the appropriate fields and determines whether the batch control is in balance before accepting the batch.
- Use of check digits. A check digit is an additional digit included in fields such as the account number. As part of the data validation program, the computer carries out a calculation on the other digits that should result in the check digit. If one of the digits has been entered incorrectly, the computation usually will not balance. The program will therefore reject most invalid account numbers.

Compensating Controls and Significance of Weaknesses

Key transcription is a necessary mechanical procedure in most ERP processing cycles. The auditor should also rely on overall user and ERP processing controls over the completeness and accuracy of ERP processing.

Many clients are relying less on key transcription controls and more on ERP validation controls to ensure the accuracy of input. If there is a weakness in key transcription controls, compensating ERP validation controls should be in effect. If there are no compensating controls, the financial information may be unreliable.

Another compensating control requires the user to sight-verify the data before it is processed. Data is entered and appears on the terminal screen or on a printout but will not be processed until the terminal operator indicates to the computer that the data has been correctly entered.

Possible Compliance Tests

- Examine written instructions and determine that they are adequate and up to date.
- Observe procedures for cancellation of input documents. Check that documents are canceled immediately after key transcription.
- Select documents from those processed during the period and examine for cancellation and evidence of key verification.

Is there editing and validation of input?

Purpose of the Controls

The purpose of controls is to prevent inaccurate or incomplete data from being accepted for processing.

Background

Checks should be built into computer programs to detect incorrect data and prevent it from being processed. These checks are known as edit and validation checks.

Control Procedures

- Format checks to ensure that each field contains either numeric or alphabetic data, depending upon its designated function.

- Missing field tests to ensure that all relevant fields have been entered.
- Limit or reasonableness checks to ensure that hourly rates do not exceed a given amount, or hours worked do not exceed hours available.
- Data field combination or correlation tests to compare the data in different fields for reasonableness based upon criteria specified in the computer program. For example, a payroll system might check that no overtime payments are made to executive staff.
- Record matching to check input transactions against related records on databases on the basis of account numbers, employee staff numbers, inventory item numbers, and so forth.
- Duplicate processing checks to identify input of duplicate sequence numbers.
- Balancing checks to ensure that certain transactions balance to zero, for example, journal entry debits and credits.
- Batch-control balancing that involves computation and agreement of control totals with batch header data.

Compensating Controls and Significance of Weaknesses

A lack of data edit and validation checks may be overcome by user or data control group controls over authorization of input, review of output, and detailed reconciliation of output to input.

Item-by-item manual verification of output can be an effective alternative user control, but it is generally inefficient.

When there are no compensating controls for weaknesses in data editing and validation, the accuracy of data accepted and processed may not be reliable. In such cases, the scope of audit procedures may need to be increased.

Possible Compliance Tests

- Obtain the listing of data rejected by the data editing and validation programs and check that the items were rejected for valid reasons.

- Review the application output for errors to confirm that data validation tests have been performed. (*Note:* This test may be less effective than the one described below. The absence of errors may indicate that no errors were present in the original data, rather than that effective data validation was performed.)
- Use computer-assisted auditing techniques, such as:
  - CAAT programs to reperform edit and validation checks.
  - Audit test data (test decks and integrated test facilities).
  - Embedded audit modules.
  - Review and testing of program coding.

ERP Processing Controls over Suspense Items

> *Are there ERP processing controls over suspense items?*

Purpose of the Controls

The purpose of controls is to ensure that suspense data is correctly identified and held pending resolution.

Background

Obtain information with regard to suspense data. How do they arise? What constitutes it? What are the company policies and procedures with respect to suspense items?

Control Procedures

- Program controls to ensure matching in subsequent processing cycles with database records and removal from suspense of matched items.
- Print out all movements both into and out of suspense records to provide a full audit trail. Movements initiated by manual means and those generated by the computer system should be indicated separately on data files and printouts.
- Update controls to ensure that the brought forward and carried forward control totals can be reconciled.

- Regular exception reports highlighting unusually high value or long-standing items.
- Regular aged analyses for all outstanding items.
- Use inquiry programs to list outstanding suspense items either completely or partially on a request basis.

Compensating Controls and Significance of Weaknesses

Scrutiny of computer listings of all suspense items following each file update is, in theory, an effective compensating control. However, if the above controls have not been properly incorporated into the computer programs, the listings may not be accurate or complete. If so, it may be necessary to use CAAT to select items for testing.

User controls over input, changes to standing data, and output can sometimes compensate for inadequately programmed controls over suspense items. If users reconcile manually developed input and cumulative control totals to output control totals; it is unlikely that material transactions erroneously held on a suspense file would remain undetected. The timeliness of compensating user controls is important to be sure that items held on suspense are recorded in the proper accounting period.

Possible Compliance Tests

- Review and test check the client's reconciliation of movements into and out of suspense records.
- Check the client's adherence to procedures for the review and follow-up of suspense items, including unusually high value or long-standing items.
- Obtain the client's list of outstanding suspense items, select items, and follow the recording of the corrected transactions and their removal from the suspense file.
- If no such list is available, use a CAAT program to report on these items.

ERP Processing Controls

Are ERP processing controls used to balance the transaction and databases?

Purpose of the Controls

The purpose of controls is to ensure that all data has been processed against the correct data files and to detect if the files are out of balance.

Background

File balancing controls can help ensure the accuracy of processing results. Control totals are established by one program and placed on a control record contained on the data file. These controls are then checked by subsequent programs to ensure that all relevant data is processed through the processing cycle.

The balancing controls will usually include checks on the header label and the control record:

- *The header label* is a record at the beginning of the file that usually contains the file name, the name of the program that created the file, the file generation number, the creation date, and the purge or scratch date (the date the file can be deleted or overwritten).
- *The control record* usually contains the total number of records and the value of all the records and hash totals held on the file. There may also be a trailer record at the end of the file containing an end of file marker and a record count.

Header and trailer label checks are generally performed by the operating system software.

Even though these control procedures are performed by the computer system, it is important that the user or the ERP control group also checks the cumulative control totals with manually developed totals.

Control Procedures

- Programmed balancing controls to check that:
  - The opening balance in the current processing cycle equals the closing balance from the previous cycle (cycle-to-cycle or run-to-run checks).
  - The opening balance plus the transactions processed equals the closing balance for the current cycle (file update controls).

- The balance, after the first program or processing step within the current cycle, equals the opening balance plus the transactions processed by the first processing step, and so on through each successive step in the system (program-to-program controls).
- The total of the individual record balances, after updating, equals the net balance in the file control record (scan and accumulate controls).

- Header label checks, under which the program reading the file confirms that the correct file has been supplied. This is done by matching the file name, program name, and creation date against data provided by the job scheduling function within the ERP processing department.
- Control record or trailer record controls, in which the program reading or processing the file independently calculates the number of records held on the file and their value. These totals are then compared with the control or trailer record to ensure that the entire file has been correctly processed.
- Prescription of procedures to be taken if the controls do not balance.

  These may be:

  - Immediate abortion of processing.
  - Reporting of discrepancies to the user for investigation while processing continues.

Compensating Controls and Significance of Weaknesses

If there are no file control records, the total number of transactions and their value should be reported after each update so that manual reconciliation can be performed. If the client has no controls over the balancing of files, the scope of audit procedures may need to be increased.

Possible Compliance Tests

- Review output listings for evidence of operation of programmed controls.
- If balancing errors have occurred, determine that the client's procedures were followed to bring the files into balance.

Is there an adequate audit trail?

Purpose of the Controls

The purpose of controls is to ensure that management can:

- Follow each transaction through the various stages of processing from the origination of the source document to each output document.
- Identify individual items included in computer totals.

Background

An adequate trail of input and generated data is important for both users and auditors. It can either be visible (printed, microfilm, or microfiche (COM—computer output to microfilm) records) or invisible (magnetic storage). In some ERP systems important totals or analyses are computed without retention of a record of the detailed computation. This loss of invisible trail frequently occurs with aged analyses of accounts receivable or provisions for accrued interest or premium income.

The availability of an audit trail will depend upon the client's retention policy for printouts, COM and source documents (for visible trail), and tape and disk files (for invisible trail). In some systems, history files of transactions are up-dated and retained on magnetic tape or disk for prescribed retention periods. However, history files are not always used. In some countries, the law requires history files and source documents to be retained for specified periods.

Control Procedures

- Identify each document by a unique sequence or batch number to facilitate tracing to and from computer output. When this identification is assigned after preparation of the source document, it should be written on the source document for cross-reference purposes.
- Process daily or periodic printouts of all input and generated transactions. These reports might include edit reports or detailed transaction listings.

- Report database control totals after updating for reconciliation by users.

When COM is used to store source documents or output, the total number of records must agree with input and output totals. This should be checked to ensure that COM is complete.

- Report the total number of records processed by programs, when complete listings of transactions processed or of items included in summary totals are not printed out.
- Clearly define retention policies for source documents, printouts, COM, and tape and disk files.

Compensating Controls and Significance of Weaknesses

When the audit trail is impaired, manual tracing of input to output may be impossible or impractical and additional audit procedures such as CAAT may be needed. In some cases, it may be possible for users and auditors to request either partial or full listings of transactions, balances, and so forth, using the client's own inquiry programs.

Possible Compliance Tests

- Determine that input documents can be traced to output reports and vice versa.
- Check that input documents and output listings are retained for an adequate period and logically filed for ease of retrieval.
- Check that procedures for allocating reference numbers to documents prevent duplication of references.

Data Control Group Controls over Input

> *Does the data control group control input?*

Purpose of the Controls

The purpose of controls is to ensure that all approved input is processed promptly through the system and that each transaction is not processed more than once.

Background

In some larger ERP installations, a separate data control function will be established. It will often be part of the ERP department and its function will be to ensure that:

- Input data is properly controlled between the user and the ERP department and within the ERP department.
- Only input from authorized sources is processed.
- Data is processed promptly.
- Output reports are distributed promptly to the correct individuals.

It is essential to ensure that data is controlled and protected against unauthorized additions or deletions from inception to final output. This may be achieved through controls imposed by users, the ERP department, or a separate data control function. From a practical viewpoint, controls imposed by a data control function will normally be considered by the auditor only when there is inadequate user control over input.

Control Procedures

- Maintain a data control log that indicates when data has been received for processing, when processing has been completed, and when output has been returned to users.
- Check batch sequence numbers for missing or duplicate batches.
- Verify that input transactions have been appropriately authorized.
- Cancel input documents to prevent duplicate processing.
- Record rejected input for subsequent follow-up and resubmission.

Compensating Controls and Significance of Weaknesses

Compensating controls may include similar procedures performed by users or by the ERP department. The computer system itself may compensate in reporting batches or documents with duplicate or missing sequence numbers.

When users, the ERP department, or a data control function do not perform such control procedures, the accuracy or completeness of data processing may not be reliable. Consequently, the scope of our audit procedures such as cut-off tests and detailed tests of transactions may need to be increased.

Possible Compliance Tests

- Trace selected batches into the data control log.
- For selected periods, check that data control has accounted for all batch numbers through all stages of processing and output.
- For selected periods, check that rejections were recorded by data control and promptly resolved.
- Confirm that procedures for reviewing authorization of input are effective.
- Test procedures for the cancellation of input documents.

Data Control Group Controls over Output

Are there control procedures within the data control group concerning review and distribution of output?

Purpose of the Controls

The purpose of controls is to ensure that the output appears reasonable and that it is properly distributed to users and third parties.

Background

After the ERP department has processed the transactions, the output reports and input documents will normally be returned directly to the data control function. The control function should ensure that processing is complete before passing the output on to users or third parties.

Control Procedures

- Reconciliation of output totals to input, cumulative data, and intermediate processing controls, prior to distribution of output. Although the user has ultimate responsibility for the completeness and accuracy of data processing, data control will normally make this preliminary reconciliation to prevent output with obvious errors from being released to users.
- Special procedures for routing confidential output to appropriate user management.
- Scrutiny of output that will be distributed directly from the data control function to third parties (e.g., sales invoices, insurance premium renewals, or payments) to detect obvious errors.

Compensating Controls and Significance of Weaknesses

Compensating controls may include similar procedures performed either by the users or the ERP department.

Possible Compliance Tests

- Check that the ERP processing control function has reconciled the output totals to input, cumulative data, and processing totals.
- Review and test check the client's reconciliation of input control totals to cumulative data and output totals.
- Observe procedures for distribution of confidential reports and scrutiny of documents distributed directly to third parties.

General Controls

Segregation of Duties and Security

Is there segregation of duties within the ERP function?

Purpose of the Controls

The purpose of controls is to ensure that members of the ERP group do not perform incompatible duties, and that the duties of one person provide a check over those performed by another.

There should also be segregation of duties between ERP group and user department staff responsible for initiation of transactions, input/output controls, maintenance of manual accounting records, and custody of assets.

Background

Segregation of duties is a fundamental element of internal control. Many frauds and thefts of data and programs have been facilitated by one employee's work never being checked by another staff member. It is particularly important that all staff be required to take their annual vacation. Other employees, taking over for employees on vacation, can provide a valuable check on their activities.

Control Procedures

- Preparation of source documents outside the ERP department.
- Restriction of access to source data submitted for processing to data entry and data control personnel.
- Prohibition of ERP group from initiating and approving transactions.
- Exclusion of ERP group from access to manually prepared accounting records, except as source documents.
- Appointment of different persons to perform the functions of:
  - ERP management.
  - ERP systems.
  - Maintenance of systems software (technical support).
  - Computer operations.
  - Data control.
  - File librarian.

- Prohibition of computer operators from making changes to programs and data. They should not have access to complete systems and program documentation.
- Prohibition of systems analysts and programmers from setting up and operating the computer, even during program testing.
- Exclusion of programmers from access to computer programs or data files that are used for production runs. When this access is considered necessary for technical reasons, it should be supervised.
- Reference checks on new employees.
- Enforcement of rotation of duties, especially for programmers, computer terminal operators, and for sensitive applications.
- Arrangements to ensure that unbroken annual vacations are taken.

Minicomputers

In very small installations, the segregation of duties outlined above is generally not feasible. The employment of additional staff to achieve further segregation of duties is not justified by the cost. The segregation of duties normally possible in such installations will be:

- ERP manager/supervisor.
- Systems analysis/programming/systems software maintenance.
- Data preparation, often outside the ERP function.
- Computer operating/file library/data control.

The need for adequate personnel procedures is increased in minicomputer environments since responsibility is concentrated in a small number of people. The departure of a key computer operator or systems analyst/programmer, combined with the lack of a knowledgeable replacement, could significantly impair the organization's continuity of ERP operations. This risk may be compensated, to some extent, by the documentation of procedures.

The inherent lack of segregation of duties may be the most significant potential internal control weakness in minicomputer installations.

Compensating Controls and Significance of Weaknesses

Where the segregation of duties is inadequate, compensating controls may exist, either within the ERP function or the user departments.
ERP function:

- Management review of the printed systems log, recording use of the computer, programs, and data files. This may compensate for control weakness caused by the failure to separate computer operations, the tape or disk library, and data control function.
- Programmed and physical restrictions on the use of input devices with respect to individual employees, transaction types, data files, and program libraries.
- Online computer editing controlled by programs so that data can be checked by users at the time of input.
- Tape or disk library records maintained by specialized software, or manually by a data control clerk.
- Application programs held permanently on disk files (program libraries).
- Programmed controls (e.g., computer-generated input totals, transaction log files, or computer file balancing with file control records).
- Provision of standard software by suppliers in object code only, not in source code, thus making unauthorized changes difficult.
- Adequate visible audit trail produced by application programs either regularly or at user request.

User department:

- Input/output reconciliations.
- Examination of detailed output, including exception reports.
- Manual signing of all negotiable documents generated by the computer.
- Manual tests of computer-generated data.
- Reconciliation of manual control records with computer file control records.

In cases where adequate segregation does not exist, the scope of audit procedures may need to be increased.

Possible Compliance Tests

- Review the organization's organization chart, concentrating on the ERP department, and discuss their responsibilities with the staff to confirm that segregation is adequate.
- Inspect evidence of supervisory review of computer systems use.
- Review personnel files to check that:
  - Adequate references were obtained.
  - Each employee took his vacation during the preceding year.
- For former operators, librarians, and programmers determine that:
  - Upon notice of termination, sensitive or confidential duties were promptly withdrawn.
  - Appropriate security measures were taken, including change of passwords, return of badges, keys, documentation, and notification to ERP and security personnel.
- Check that duties are rotated regularly.

Are there controls that restrict unauthorized physical access to the computer room, terminals, tape and disk files, databases, and systems and programming documentation?

Purpose of the Controls

The purpose of controls is to minimize the risk of unauthorized physical access, resulting in:

- Accidental or deliberate disclosure of confidential information.
- Accidental or deliberate modification of data files or programs.
- Accidental or deliberate destruction of data, programs, or equipment.

- Theft of data, programs, or equipment.
- Unauthorized computer use.

Background

Access controls may be exercised by physical means or by software checks. Physical restrictions include electronic surveillance methods, magnetic card locks, security guards, key locks, and so forth. The exact method to be used should be decided after an assessment of the sensitivity and value of the data, programs and equipment, and the cost-effectiveness of the various methods. Software checks are most often used to control access from online terminals to data files and program libraries.

Control Procedures

- Access to the computer room restricted to those people required for the functioning of computer operations.
- Special arrangements to cover access by visitors, outside contractors, maintenance engineers, and cleaners.
- Secure location of computer room, systems and programming areas, and backup file storage area.
- Procedures and records to control the issue and return of physical access devices, such as keys, magnetic cards, lock combinations, electronic transmitters, and identification badges.
- Notification to ERP management and security personnel when staff leave the organization's employment.
- Restriction of access to on-site terminals to authorized employees.
- Controls over access to data files and programs, including:
  - Recording of tape and disk usage and inventory.
  - Recording of issue from and return to the computer operations area of tapes and disks.

Normally, only larger computer installations can justify the cost of employing a full-time tape and disk librarian with no responsibility for operating the computer. In smaller installations, this should be the part-time responsibility of someone other than the operator, for example the data control clerk or the IT supervisor.

- Prescription of the same access controls for all shifts. If this is not the case, there should be an acceptable alternative such as:
  - Pre-issue (job set-up) of tape and disk files for night and weekend shifts in accordance with approved job schedules.
  - Attendance of at least one supervisor in the computer operations area during all shifts.
  - Restrictions on access to systems, program, and operating documentation. In some installations, a secure copy of such documentation may be held either on microfilm or microfiche records, or as part of a program library on disk with software access protection.
- Restriction of access to input devices by physical locks and programmed password checks.

Minicomputers

Most minicomputers have input devices that enable direct access to data files for inquiry or update. Different levels of passwords may be used to restrict access for different purposes. Strict security over passwords should be maintained; passwords should be changed at irregular intervals and upon departure of operators.

Physical security of a minicomputer installation is normally more difficult to control because the equipment is often located within the user's department and not in a separate computer room. However, it should be checked that:

- The minicomputer is sited away from areas of public access.
- The minicomputer location is supervised.
- The equipment is not left unattended when switched on.

Compensating Controls and Significance of Weaknesses

Where there are weak physical access controls, it will be necessary to rely on compensating controls, such as:

- User controls over the completeness and accuracy of ERP processing.

- Backup facilities for equipment, data files, programs, documentation, and people, to cover disruption of ERP processing.
- Controls over unauthorized operating of the computer and records of computer use.

When weaknesses in physical access controls are not compensated for, it may not be possible to rely on the accuracy of processing results. It may be necessary to increase the scope of audit procedures, possibly using CAAT. A lack of control over unauthorized disclosure of confidential data and programs is difficult to compensate for, but this is unlikely to have direct audit significance, unless the data is exceptionally valuable.

Possible Compliance Tests

- Observe the physical control over access to the computer room, tape library, databases, input documents, input data files, and program documentation.
- Obtain lists of those having access to each area within the computer installation. Confirm that these lists are authorized.
- Check that systems and program documentation is available only to authorized employees.
- Test recording and authorization for issues and returns of tape and disk files to and from the library.
- Obtain lists of all terminals and consider the physical security of each location. Test that terminals are locked or inaccessible to unauthorized persons when not in use. Determine that only authorized persons possess keys or know the passwords.
- Discuss the security procedures for night and weekend shifts with operators and security personnel to determine the adequacy of the arrangements.

Controls over Systems Software

Are there controls over changes to systems software?

Purpose of the Controls

The purpose of controls is to ensure that only authorized versions of systems software are used.

Background

Systems software is typically acquired from and maintained by computer manufacturers or software houses. It includes:

- Operating systems, which coordinate the use of computer equipment, data files, and programs, and often permit more than one program to run concurrently.
- Utility programs, which assist in computer operations such as sorting, copying, or dumping, or, which assist programmers in making changes to data files or programs. The latter programs often leave no audit trail and should be closely controlled.
- Communications monitors, which handle communication between the computer and online terminals.
- Database management systems, which control the organization of, access to, and completeness and accuracy of a database.
- Language translators (compilers), which are used to convert programs from one computer language into another, often from source code into object code.
- Program library software, which is used for storing source and object programs, restricting access to program libraries, monitoring authorized program changes, and reporting program inventory, use, and changes.
- Data file access protection software, which is used for identification of users, authorization of data file processing, and monitoring and logging of unauthorized file access attempts.

A person who can change systems software may have opportunities to initiate unauthorized transactions, and to modify application programs and data files. However, systems software is complex, and usually only supplied in object code. Consequently, only a highly skilled technician will have the ability to change it.

The systems software installed and the control features of audit significance provided should be known. Changes made to purchased software, and their impact on controls, should be investigated. The organization's procedures to minimize the possibilities of bypassing the automated controls should also be determined.

Control Procedures

- Segregation of the software function (technical support group) from other ERP functions, especially application programming. There should be a separate group of programmers responsible for the acquisition, modification, and maintenance of systems software.
- Procedures for the administration and control of the software function.
- Authorization of the addition of utilities to the program library.
- Incorporation of security and file access features into the systems software.
- Authorization, testing, and documenting of in-house modifications to systems software. The results of testing should be reviewed by someone other than the person who initiated the modification.
- Tight control over the use of utilities that enable programs, terminal assignments, operating systems, or data files to be changed without leaving an audit trail. This should include:
  - Restricting availability of these utilities to the smallest possible number of users.
  - Recording of all users by the systems software.
  - ERP management review and approval of the results of their use.
  - Password controls.

Minicomputers

In general, systems software available for minicomputers is not as comprehensive as for mainframe installations. There will also be fewer automated controls provided over computer use, data and program file use, recovery facilities, and internal file label checks. While most mini-computer suppliers do provide utility programs that enable users to make online program changes, these programs generally have fewer automated controls.

Compensating Controls and Significance of Weaknesses

Even with the above controls, a highly skilled person, knowledgeable in all aspects of an application system, including programmed and user controls, may be able to change programs and data files without leaving any evidence of such changes. There are few individual control procedures that can specifically prevent or detect this. However, strong user and programmed controls over individual applications, combined with adequate ERP department management and supervision, can greatly reduce the risk.

Possible Compliance Tests

- Determine that the system programmers are independent of other ERP functions by reviewing the organization charts and by observation.
- Where the organization has implemented new, or has modified existing, systems software, obtain the record of changes, select changes, and review:
  - The approval for making the change.
  - The tests performed to ensure that the software functions correctly.
  - The final approval that the change was made correctly.
- Determine proper authorization of the use of any utilities that enable programs, terminal assignments, operating systems, or data files to be changed without leaving an audit trail, by reviewing the output of the job accounting system. Note that such utilities may be renamed and, consequently, their identity may not be obvious.
- Determine how the organization prohibits bypassing the security and file access controls of the systems software and check that this prohibition is effective.

Controls over Operations

> **Are there procedures to minimize the risk that unauthorized jobs and programs are run?**

Purpose of the Controls

The purpose of controls is to ensure that there is no unauthorized use of the computer facility.

Background

In addition to the controls over physical access to computer facilities, a job accounting system is an important management tool to help prevent unauthorized runs. This is a computer program that records what jobs were run, how much time they required, and other information pertinent to each program used. If there is no job accounting system, controls can be established by using manually prepared operator logs or by reviewing the computer console logs. These alternatives are much less efficient than an automated job accounting system because they include a lot of other information, and are more difficult to read and summarize.

Control Procedures

- Recording of information regarding which jobs have been processed. This should be available from one or more of the following:
  - A computerized job accounting system.
  - A console log.
  - A console terminal screen, backed up by a disk or tape systems log with selective printing.
- Review of this information by management to determine that:
  - Jobs were run in accordance with the job schedule.
  - Specified operating procedures were followed.
  - Periods of idle time or down-time are explained.
- Prescribed retention periods for console logs or job accounting system records.

- Procedures to prevent suppression of information on which jobs have been processed
- Job scheduling procedures.
- Periodic analysis and control of computer use by application, showing production, re-run, repair, maintenance, idle time, and so forth.
- Submission of a regular summary of computer use to senior management for review and approval.
- Maintenance of manual logs by computer operators and their review by management. This procedure is generally less satisfactory than the use of an automated logging procedure.

Minicomputers

Because of the lack of segregation of duties in minicomputer installations, computer operations and use are more difficult to control. The systems software provided will often not include job accounting systems or console logs.

Compensating Controls and Significance of Weaknesses

The control procedures should be evaluated in the context of the size of the installation, including number of staff, number of tapes and disks stored, and size of computer configuration. If the controls are weak, the adequacy of access controls should be assessed. If neither access nor operations controls are satisfactory, it may not be possible to rely on the programmed application controls.

Possible Compliance Tests

- Examine job accounting system reports or the printed console logs and test:
  - Sequence, to check that all computer time is accounted for.
  - Evidence of approval by management.
  - Appropriate action taken.
- Check that a summary of computer use has been submitted to and approved by senior management.

- Determine whether users receive output reports on time. Confirm that significant delays are reported to management; obtain explanations.

Are there controls that ensure the use of the correct tape and disk files?

Purpose of the Controls

The purpose of controls is to prevent the processing of incorrect data files.

Background

Computer programs access data files for information retrieval, processing, matching, and update. If the wrong tape or disk file is used the output will be incorrect and data could be lost.

Control Procedures

- Use of specialized software (tape and disk library management system) to control the use of files. This may be part of the operating system or a separate software package.
- Use of standard internal header labels for all tape and disk files.
- Maintenance of reference and control data on header labels. This may include file name, volume serial number, and creation and expiration dates.
- Checking of correct tape or disk file labels by application programs and the operating system. Checking of internal file labels by system software is not available in all minicomputer installations. Prevent operators from overriding standard label checks.
- Inclusion of sufficient information in the job set-up to indicate which version of a file should be used.
- External labeling of files and checks by operators in conjunction with the manual file library records. This may be an alternative to programmed controls.

Compensating Controls and Significance of Weaknesses

Compensating controls may include:

- Adequate audit trail of control totals and generated data.
- Data file balancing controls performed by the application programs or user departments. A data control function may also undertake an initial manual balancing check.
- Testing of computer output by user departments.

It is rare to encounter a situation where weaknesses in controls over proper file use are not compensated by some form of balancing procedure. If, however, such a situation does occur, the risk of inaccurate processing is high and additional audit procedures will probably be required.

Possible Compliance Tests

- Test job set-up and operating instructions to confirm that there is a clear indication of which version of a tape or disk file is to be used.
- Print header labels for selected files and check the information held.
- Review the console log or job accounting system for evidence of overrides of the automatic label check.

Is there supervision of computer operations staff for all shifts?

Purpose of the Controls

The purpose of controls is to minimize the risk of errors or irregularities arising from computer operations.

Background

The organization of the ERP function should include effective supervision of each level of activity, including operations, tape and disk library, data control, data preparation, and job scheduling. An important area to consider is shift changeover.

Control Procedures

- Clearly defined reporting and supervising responsibilities ideally described an organization chart.
- Attendance by management during all shifts.
- Control scheduling of jobs to be run each shift.
- Formalized shift changeover procedures. There should be a written record so that persons on the new shift know what has or has not been done on the prior shift. This should include lists of jobs in process, their status, and reports of systems software problems.
- Operator program run instructions (run-books), including:
  - Details of job set-up instructions.
  - JCL (job control) instructions.
  - Console messages requiring operator action and the operator's responses.
  - Action to be taken in case of failure to run a job.
  - End of job instructions.

In many installations job set-up is simplified by using cataloged JCL procedures.

Minicomputers

Frequently, in smaller installations there is only one operator who performs all ERP functions for second or third shifts. In such an environment, it is not cost-effective to have a supervisor available for each shift.

Compensating Controls and Significance of Weaknesses

If supervisory controls are inadequate, the following controls over the completeness and accuracy for individual applications should be considered:

- Adequacy of audit trail of control totals and generated data.
- Data file balancing performed by the application programs or user departments. An initial manual balancing check may also be undertaken by a data control function.
- Testing of computer output by user departments.

Management controls may be applied to compensate for the lack of supervision. If there is proper use and review of job accounting system reports and console logs, the absence of supervision may be less important.

Possible Compliance Tests

- Examine the computer operator run-book and check that it is adequate.
- Check that the operator runs the jobs as prescribed by the run-book.
- Examine the shift roster to confirm that management is present on each shift.

Controls over Continuity of Processing

> *Are there procedures to prevent a disaster affecting the ERP function from causing a major disruption to the information flow or a loss of accounting control?*
>
> *Is the documentation of the ERP function adequate to ensure that the organization can continue in operation if an important ERP group left its employment?*

Purpose of the Controls

The purpose of controls is to ensure the continuity of ERP processing, that accounting records can be recreated in the event of disaster, and that operations can proceed in the event of the departure of key employees.

Background

Major disruption of the ERP function in an organization that is highly reliant on ERP could lead to significant disruption of its business operations, cash flow, management information, and accounting records. In extreme cases, the viability of the organization as a going concern could be endangered.

Major disruption may be brought about by:

- Failure of hardware.
- Failure of software. This can occur when a program is unable to handle a particular situation, for example, an unusual type of input.
- Failure of electrical power supply, air-conditioning, or cooling water supply.
- Destruction of equipment, data files, or programs.
- Loss of teleprocessing facilities.
- Loss of an installation's only copy of systems and program documentation.
- Strikes or resignations by key staff, especially computer operators, programmers, and data preparation clerks.

Control Procedures

- Establishment and periodic testing of disaster recovery procedures, such as:
  - Fire precautions.
  - Backup electrical power.
  - Standby processing, for both the computer equipment and the terminal network.
- Regular maintenance by the manufacturer or some other competent service organization.
- Retention of at least three cycles of master files, commonly referred to as grandfather, father, and son.
- Remote (off-site) storage for copies of:
  - Master files.
  - Transaction files.
  - Documentation (systems, program, operator, and user).
  - Computer programs.
- Establishment of priorities for applications to be processed by standby facilities.

- Maintenance of up-to-date installation manuals, which include:
  - Systems descriptions.
  - Authorities, dates, and details of system modifications.
  - Narrative descriptions (specifications) of each program.
  - Program flowcharts, decision tables, or other documents showing the logic and decision steps involved in each program.
  - Current source code program listings.
  - Test data, results, and approvals.
  - ERP processing procedures, including data preparation, data control, computer operations, tape and disk library, and terminal operations.
- Cross-training of staff to provide backup.

Minicomputers

Security against destruction of equipment, data files, and programs, and provision for continuous operations is as important for minicomputers as for larger installations. Arrangements to ensure that the ERP function can continue in operation if a key employee leaves are of particular significance in minicomputer installations. Because most minicomputer installations have a small staff, there is an increased vulnerability to departure of a key systems analyst/programmer or operator.

Compensating Controls and Significance of Weaknesses

In assessing the impact of a major disruption to the ERP function, whether the following factors provide any degree of compensation should be considered:

- Ability to continue in business and maintain control without the computer.
- Ability to convert certain applications to non-ERP operation.
- Arrangement of priority standby processing for the most critical systems.
- Adequate insurance cover for the cost of physical assets, for reconstructing data, and for loss of business.

- Distribution of ERP processing among several computer installations, as opposed to one or two large units.

Applications using acquired software packages can sometimes be processed at a third party's installation using the latter's software and the organization's own backup data files.

Poor documentation may be less important if there are several analysts and programmers on the staff who were involved with the development of the application.

Generally, unless a disaster occurs, weaknesses in these controls will not have an impact on the audit. However, the effect that a disaster might have on the organization's ability to continue in business should be assessed. Weaknesses should be brought to the attention of organization management.

Possible Compliance Tests

It is generally not necessary to carry out any compliance testing on these controls. In some circumstances it may be important to:

- Determine whether there is any written disaster recovery procedures and assess their adequacy.
- Review evidence of the procedures having been tested and the results of the tests.
- Determine how the organization ensures that the procedures remain viable and effective.
- Visit the off-premises storage facility and determine for selected applications that important transaction files, master files, computer programs, and documentation are there and whether this information is sufficient to enable recovery. Select some files for subsequent printing of internal labels.
- In connection with audit procedures concerning insurance:
  - Confirm cover with insurers.
  - Examine policies.
  - Review adequacy of cover.
- Examine the systems design and programming standards manual to determine that the manual prescribes reasonable standards for documentation.

- Examine the documentation for selected applications and determine that:
  - The documentation permits the organization to continue processing data if an important ERP group leaves.
  - The documentation contains a description of the system, including narratives, program flowchart, system flowchart, output, user requirements, controls, and so forth.
- The documentation indicates who performed maintenance changes, including systems analysis, programming, and updating of the program library.

  - The documentation includes a current source code compilation listing with necessary cross-references.

Controls over Application Systems Development

> *Is there user involvement in the modifications to existing systems?*

Purpose of the Controls

The purpose of controls is to ensure that the system modifications satisfy the users' requirements.

Background

An error in program or system design can have pervasive effects and be costly to correct. Consequently, computer systems should be developed and implemented in a controlled manner with active user involvement to help ensure that they are reliable and meet the users' needs. More organizations are now purchasing ERP systems. The procedures for user involvement and testing of these systems should be similar to those for systems developed by the organization.

Control Procedures

- Preparation by the user of a formal statement of requirements.
- Approval by the user of the feasibility study and outline system proposals.

- Approval by the user of the detailed system design, including system specifications. It is important that user management approves the system design and controls before program implementation. In the case of advanced systems, the development work will often be done in stages, and specifications for each stage should be drafted and submitted to user management separately.
- Documentation of user controls. User controls are often documented after a system has been fully implemented. It is best to prescribe and document user controls prior to the parallel running or systems acceptance testing, so that they can be tested at the same time.
- Approval by the user of the results of parallel running or systems accepting tests prior to implementation. Parallel running is sometimes not feasible or cost-effective. In this case, comprehensive testing of the new system (acceptance testing) must be relied upon.
- Checking of initial data file creation and reconciliation of opening control totals with previous system records.
- Authorization by the users of modifications to system design. For many organizations, the major programming effort is devoted to making maintenance changes to existing systems. These changes may result from user requests, ERP processing requests, or external events such as tax law changes. The controls over changes should be similar to the controls for new systems and should include user involvement in acceptance testing and updated documentation.
- Retention by users of an up-to-date copy of the system specifications or a comprehensive user manual.
- Authorization and recording of users' changes to look-up tables or parameters included in programs.
- Review by the users of documentation and assessment of controls included in software packages acquired from third parties.

Minicomputers

In general, the procedures for controlling the implementation and modification of minicomputer systems should be similar to those for larger installations. The following are particular points to consider with mini-computer installations:

- *Purchased programs.* Often minicomputer application systems are purchased from smaller manufacturers or software houses that may not be familiar with online system control techniques. Before programs are purchased, the system should be reviewed to ensure it meets the same standards as for in-house development. Particular areas of concern include:
  - ○ Processing controls such as edit, data logging, and file balancing routines.
  - ○ System testing.
  - ○ User approval before acceptance.
  - ○ Documentation to provide information to allow maintenance of the applications.
- *Modifications to existing programs.* Because of the small number of people involved in the minicomputer installation and the lack of segregation of duties, control over modifications to existing programs is very important.
- *Documentation.* Documentation is important in all ERP areas. In minicomputer installations, it becomes even more so because of the relatively small number of employees involved. Assigning an employee outside the computer function responsibility for ensuring that adequate documentation exists should be consideered. The organization may not be knowledgeable about ERP processing standards and documentation and may wish to call on outsiders, such as its auditors, to review the standards periodically and to check that documentation is adequate.

Compensating Controls and Significance of Weaknesses

In practice, even without user involvement in systems implementation, the systems analysts may adequately consider the needs of users and internal control; and the implemented system may perform effectively.

In addition, participation by users in system testing and imple-mentation may prove adequate even if they are not involved in the ear-lier stages of the project.

When user controls are designed to detect unauthorized or erroneous changes to old systems or errors in new systems, lack of written procedures is not a critical weakness from an audit viewpoint.

Possible Compliance Tests

- Review the written specifications for new applications.
- Test written specifications for modifications to existing applications. Determine whether the specifications were prepared in accordance with the installation standards.
- Check that the user is satisfied that the specifications incorporate all user requirements.
- Determine, by discussion with users and ERP group, the extent of modification to significant accounting applications during the year and whether they reflect adequate user participation in system development.

Are there testing procedures for new systems and modifications to existing systems?

Purpose of the Controls

The purpose of controls is to ensure that new systems and modifications to existing systems are operating satisfactorily before they are implemented.

Background

If adequate testing is not carried out, it is likely that the system will not function properly, especially in its initial processing periods. Accordingly, the system may require numerous corrections. In addition to the primary system, it is important that all sub-routines are tested comprehensively. In the case of acquired software packages, the organization should perform testing similar to that done for systems developed in-house.

Control Procedures

- Prescription of detailed testing procedures.
- Use of comprehensive test data files.
- Use of test data files only, not live production files.
- Complete system testing, including testing interactions between programs.
- Testing of user and ERP processing input/output controls.
- Spot-checks of program tests and coding by programming management.
- Input of test data by system users and assessment of test results by them.
- Parallel running or acceptance testing prior to implementation.
- Retention of test data and results for subsequent use in system maintenance.

Compensating Controls and Significance of Weaknesses

In general, comprehensive testing of new systems is highly desirable. However, in practice a system may perform satisfactorily without full testing. If, on the other hand, there is evidence of numerous modifications to a new system, output for the period when the system first became operational should be carefully examined.

In the absence of adequate testing procedures, the users need to determine that ERP processing applications are producing accurate results. Testing is an extremely important preventive control that helps assure that programs accomplish their objectives. In the case of an acquired software package, any information available on the package and the results of any previous evaluation should be considered.

Possible Compliance Tests

- For selected applications, check that adequate testing was performed.
- Confirm that the results of the tests were reviewed by ERP and user management.

- In case of system modifications, determine that not only the individual program modified, but also the entire system, including sections not changed, is tested.
- Confirm that adequate parallel running and acceptance testing was performed before the system went into production.
- Check that the parallel running and acceptance testing included user controls.

Are there implementation procedures for new systems and modifications to existing systems?

Purpose of the Controls

The purpose of controls is to ensure that the implementation of new or revised systems is carried out properly, to minimize the risk of errors not being detected.

Background

Implementation procedures include the documentation, approval, and installation of new software and related user and ERP processing controls. They also include procedures necessary to ensure that existing records held on transaction and master files are reordered, or translated properly so they can be processed by the new system. This reordering or translation is termed *data conversion.*

Control Procedures

- Formal sign-off approval by users of results of system testing.
- Written authority by either ERP or user management to catalog new or modified programs in the production program library, and to remove old programs.
- Reporting by the computer system of all changes made to programs and program libraries.
- Verification by user or ERP management that all changes were authorized and applied correctly.

- Completion and updating of all relevant documentation.
- Appropriate training for ERP and user staff.
- Procedures for the conversion of data from the previous to the new system, including:
  - Reconciliation of control totals.
  - User tests of individual balances and items of standing data on a printout of the converted file.
- Use of program library software that monitors program changes for authorization and that records program identities, versions, use, status, and number of source documents.

Are there implementation procedures for new systems and modifications to existing systems?

Compensating Controls and Significance of Weaknesses

If adequate implementation controls are not effected, there is the possibility of error in the period when the system first becomes operational. There is also the possibility of error in data conversion when the new system requires structural change to master and transaction files. To overcome this, testing of the period following conversion may need to be increased. Testing the error correction and conversion procedures is especially important.

Assessment of the significance of weaknesses in implementation controls often depends on when the conversion occurs. If a conversion takes place at the beginning of the financial year, most errors will probably have been corrected by the end of the period being audited. For example, customers will have complained and their account balances will have been corrected. However, if the conversion occurs relatively close to a year-end, errors may not be corrected before the year-end. Thus, a conversion close to a year-end may require increased testing of the conversion or increased substantive testing, such as accounts receivable confirmations.

Adequate controls over implementation of new systems and modifications to existing systems permit reliance on programmed controls for accounting applications. If controls over these changes are weak, the degree of assurance provided over input and output by user controls will have to be considered. The programmed controls will often depend on the relative complexity of the system design.

Possible Compliance Tests

- Determine that the user approved the new systems before they went into operation.
- Confirm that written approval was given to catalog new or revised programs for production.
- Check that the total of the files at the end of the old system is equal to the total of the files at the beginning of the new system.
- Test individual items from the new system to the old system and vice versa.
- Confirm that the file conversion has been reviewed and approved by the user.
- Confirm that the systems documentation, including user controls, was completed and available before the system became operational.
- Determine that provision was made for training of ERP and user department staff prior to implementation of the new application.
- Confirm that controls over access to the program library are adequate. If a program library software package is used, test the log of program changes for authorization.

Controls for Advanced ERP Systems

Online Input Controls

Are there controls to restrict online terminal use to authorized persons?

Purpose of the Controls

The purpose of controls is to prevent unauthorized access to, use of, and changes to computer programs and data.

Background

Controls over physical access to computer installations and over the running of unauthorized programs have already been discussed. In on-line systems, restrictions over use of the computer terminals to prevent unauthorized access to data and programs are important.

It is also important to guard against unauthorized access through remote access that permits entry of data from remote locations.

The most common procedure used to achieve this objective is some form of access security code or password. In order to use remote access, an operator will have to input a password that will be checked by the computer. Frequently, different passwords will be used to control different types of terminal use.

It is not always possible to prevent unauthorized access by a person with sufficient expertise, resourcefulness, and determination. Therefore, senior management must consider the degree of risk associated with the data it wishes to protect and the costs of feasible alternative protection procedures. In making this decision, management must consider the adequacy of compensating user controls over input and output.

Control Procedures

- Master lists of persons authorized remote access with indicated restrictions on use.
- Issue of passwords or other forms of user identification for verification by the computer system.
- Restrictions to a limited range of activity by terminal operators. For example, operators should only be able to use specified terminals for appropriate purposes. Access should be restricted to relevant data files, individual records, data fields within records, and specified programs. In some cases, operators may be restricted to inquiries with no up-date facility.
- Prevention of display of confidential data on terminal screens and printouts.
- Maintenance of security over passwords, including:
  ○ Personal recording and retention by individual operators.
  ○ Terminal display protection. Passwords should not be displayed on the terminal screen or printout.

- ○ Clearly defined responsibility for issuing and changing passwords.
- ○ Frequent changing.
- ○ Use of passwords in combination. For example, employee identity plus password, physical locks plus password.
- Encryption (security coding) of data during transmission and on files.
- Specified signing on and signing off procedures that are verified by the computer system. Some systems software provides for terminals to be automatically locked in the event of suspicious activity, or if the terminal has not been used for a specified period. This latter procedure should help prevent take over by an unauthorized user when an authorized user stops.
- Physical security of terminal locations, maintained by mechanical devices, equipment locks, and so forth.
- Monitoring of terminal activity by the use of automated access logs that record all activity and report on rejected or suspicious attempts to use the terminal.

Compensating Controls and Significance of Weaknesses

Unauthorized updates of data files should be exposed by adequate user input/output reconciliations if there is a segregation of user duties and an adequate audit trail.

The exposure of unauthorized online program changes will depend on:

- Controls over documentation and cataloging of program changes.
- Segregation of duties between ERP and user staff.
- User controls over input and output, including the agreement of master file control totals and an adequate audit trail.

Possible Compliance Tests

- Review the list of authorized users to confirm that there is adequate segregation of duties between users and programmers, and within the user departments.

- Obtain a list of all terminals by location and consider physical security. Test that terminals are kept locked or protected in some other way from unauthorized use.
- Observe logging-on procedures and note the functioning of password verification. Check that confidentiality is respected. For example, passwords are not shown on the screen or in the user manual.
- Review the terminal access log and check that failed access attempts of a suspicious nature have been investigated.
- Check that passwords are changed upon departure or transfer of staff.
- Determine how often all passwords are changed and who has authority to change them.

Is there balancing of control totals for online input?

Purpose of the Controls

The purpose of controls is to ensure the complete and accurate entry of data into online systems, using control totals reconciled by users from data entry, through successive processing stages to master file/database updates.

Background

The three principal types of online systems are described in Chapter 1.

Control Procedures

Online inquiry, with batch-controlled data entry for both transaction, masterfiles, and databases

- Use of conventional batch control procedures.

Online data capture

- Establishment of control totals for subsequent reporting and reconciliation by a user not involved in data entry or in authorization of transactions. This should be done:

- As the data is entered. Separate control totals should be established for each terminal and for each transaction type. This may be done either manually or by the input device.
- At the end of the day. The computer should record the total of the items accumulated on the transaction file.
- After updating the master file. This may include:
  - An update of master file control records produced using the control record on the transaction file.
  - A programmed accumulation of the individual master file records for reconciliation with the master file control record.
  - A master file/database update report showing total balances brought forward, today's total movements by transaction type, and total balances carried forward.

Real time update

- Maintenance of a transaction log file, independent of the master file, that records all transactions entered directly to the master file for each shift's or day's processing.
- Recording all data generated and updated directly by the system on the transaction log file. This data may be depreciation provisions, insurance premium renewals, or direct debits.
- Establishment of control totals by the computer each shift or day for:
- Input data, by type of transaction and terminal.
- Generated data, by type of data.
- Recording of a transaction summary by the computer system, at the end of a shift or day, on both the transaction log file and on the master file.
- Maintenance of a master file control record including:
  - The totals of all opening balances at the start of each shift or day.
  - A summary of transactions posted from the transaction log file.
  - The totals of all closing balances at the end of each shift or day. This should equal the aggregate of the previous two items.

The total movements for each shift or day as reported in the control records should be printed in a master file update report for balancing by the user.

Compensating Controls and Significance of Weaknesses

It is difficult to compensate for a lack of control over input entered through online terminals and remote access. If the audit trail of control totals is inadequate, it should be determined if controls over individual items entered are strong enough to compensate for the potential weaknesses in control totals. Causes of inadequate control totalling may include:

- A management decision that clerically maintained or computer-generated input totals are not cost-effective.
- A real time system design that does not provide for a transaction log file and programmed balancing with the master file.

When there is a potential weakness caused by an absence of control totals, the types of transactions being entered and their significance in the context of the financial statements should be considered. For example, in systems where customer orders are entered for subsequent generation of shipping documents and invoices by the computer, it may not be necessary to establish manual totals for orders entered. Instead it may be possible to rely on:

- A transaction log of accepted orders and computer-generated totals.
- Subsequent programmed matching of accepted orders, shipping documents, and invoices.
- Subsequent programmed reconciliation of total orders with shipping documents, invoices, and the master file update.

Possible Compliance Tests

Online inquiry with batch controlled data entry for both transaction and master files

- Test batch control procedures.

Online data capture

- If the input control totals are recorded in a control register, test the procedures as for batch controls.
- If users do not maintain input control totals, test completeness of input as follows.
  - For a sample of input documents, check input to a printed transaction log or by using a terminal screen inquiry facility.
  - Verify the accuracy of the transaction log totals generated by the system, by manual addition or the use of CAAT.
  - Check the transaction log totals to the master file update report and vice versa.
  - Select file update reports and confirm evidence of user procedures in conjunction with testing of user controls over output.
- If there is no visible trail of computer-generated control totals and automated file balancing use CAAT to:
  - Check the accuracy of control records on the transaction log and master file.
  - Determine whether the transaction log is complete for a sample of input documents.
  - Simulate file balancing errors using test data and check proper reporting by the computer system.

Real time update

- Where control totals are maintained either by the user or by the computer, carry out tests as for online data capture.

Is there an adequate audit trail of individual items entered for processing using online terminals?

Purpose of the Controls

The purpose of controls is to provide a record of transactions entered for processing.

Background

The subject of audit trail is discussed in general terms in Chapter 3. It is particularly important that management be able to trace the source of input in online applications. This question highlights the most significant additional control procedures for online applications.

Control Procedures

- Sequential numbering of items by the computer system with identifying codes for each transaction entered from each terminal.
- Confirmation of individual items of input or groups of items transmitted back to the terminals for display or printing.
- Periodic or ad hoc printouts of processed items with control totals.
- Monitoring of items processed by the computer system by using statistical sampling or exception reporting of items, such as missing serial numbers, abnormal items, or duplicated items.
- Use of message headers and end-of-transmission trailers to verify that all items have been transmitted correctly.
- Maintenance of transaction log files.

Compensating Controls and Significance of Weaknesses

We are likely to encounter the following control weaknesses:

- An absence of source documents for certain types of input, such as customer orders.
- Failure to maintain a transaction log file, especially in some software packages for minicomputers.
- A lack of programmed sequence checks on prenumbered input documents.
- Display of data on screens only with no hard copy output retained, especially in minicomputer applications.

There are few compensating controls for an inadequate trail of individual items. However, where there is an absence of source documents, daily computer listings of items entered (both accepted and rejected), when combined with sequence number checks and subsequent authorization by management, may provide adequate audit evidence.

Possible Compliance Tests

- Confirm that procedures for assigning sequence identification numbers to documents prevent duplication.
- Observe terminal input *dialogue* to confirm that:
  - The user receives confirmation of each item entered.
  - The user marks the computer-generated sequence identification number on the source document itself or has other procedures that allow for cross-referencing to computer-generated transaction listings.
  - The system checks against duplicate entries.
- Confirm that the system checks for missing sequence numbers on prenumbered input documents by a review of exception reports. Or, check the completeness of sequence numbers by a review of output reports or by use of CAAT.

Recovery and Restart for Online Systems

> *Are there recovery and restart procedures in the event of online transmission or processing failure?*

Purpose of the Controls

The purpose of controls is to ensure continuity and reliability of ERP processing in the event of short-term failure.

Background

Both continuity and reliability of processing are at risk when computer hardware or software fails during ERP processing. Although this is true in all computer systems, it is more critical in online applications. In these systems, an interruption in processing can result in the loss of transactions or may make it difficult to determine transactions that were or were not processed before the interruption. This can be especially serious when there is no hard copy source document for reference.

ERP log files are usually used in conjunction with cyclic copying (dumping) of master files to help ensure effective recovery and restart procedures. This ERP log (which may be the same as the file access and transaction logs discussed previously) is used to update the restored master files with transactions entered since the last dumping of the master files. It may sometimes be part of the same physical logs used for file access and transactions. It may be accessed automatically by the recovery features provided in some advanced systems software.

Control Procedures

- Maintenance of magnetic tape or disk ERP logs by the computer system recording all items entered and inquiries made. The data written to the ERP log is comprised of:
  - Terminal identification.
  - Date and time.
  - Transaction identification.
  - Identification of program used.
  - Password.
  - Terminal operator personal identification.
  - Message serial number. A serial number is added to each message, either by the terminal operator or by the computer system, to facilitate identification and tracing.
  - Identification of the record retrieved or modified.
  - Name of the modified field for each modified record (keyword).
  - The changed records, both before and after update.
- Periodic or ad hoc printing of ERP logs in order to identify the processing steps completed for individual items.
- Procedures for the re-creation of master file data in the event of loss or destruction. This may involve:
  - Cyclic dumping (copying) of master files onto tape or disk. At prescribed intervals, the contents of files created or

modified since the previous dump are copied. The frequency of dumping should be determined on the basis of volumes, sensitivity of data, frequency of processing, and so forth.

- ○ Retention of all transaction files and input documents before making the most recent copy of the master file.
- Definition of retention periods for duplicate master files and transaction files.
- Periodic testing of automatic recovery procedures.
- Sequential numbering of input items by the computer system to aid identification and recovery.
- Update of a duplicate master file simultaneously with the main file. This is an alternative to cyclic dumping in some online applications.
- Graceful degradation procedures. It is usually difficult to provide cost-effective complete backup processing facilities for a network of online terminals. But, it is desirable to provide ERP processing capability to the fullest extent possible. The procedures for providing a partial service are commonly referred to as *graceful degradation* and may include:
  - ○ Advice to terminal locations of failure and corrective action.
  - ○ Automatic shutdown of the faulty device and transfer to an alternative functioning unit.
  - ○ Transfer to a standby electricity generator.
  - ○ Provision of file inquiries but no file updating.
  - ○ Transfer of input data onto magnetic files for subsequent processing on the computer after it has become operational or for dispatch to another computer installation for batch processing.
  - ○ A switch from leased telephone lines to the public network.
  - ○ Transfer of the whole system to another computer. This is only exceptionally required.
- Reversion to offline batch processing at a central computer installation. This is usually required only in the event of a prolonged disruption.

Compensating Controls and Significance of Weaknesses

There are no fully effective compensating controls with respect to the ability to continue processing. However, strong user controls over data entered will reduce the risk of incomplete or inaccurate processing.

Possible Compliance Tests

- Determine the frequency of system failures, and the level of user understanding of and satisfaction with recovery procedures, through monitoring logs and discussion with ERP and user staff.
- Check that proper recovery procedures were followed for selected days on which system failures occurred.
- Check that recovery procedures have been clearly defined, documented, and tested if no system failures have occurred.
- Check that ERP logs are reviewed and retained and that copies of master files are kept as prescribed.

Controls over Online Program Changes

> *Are there controls over online program changes?*

Purpose of the Controls

The purpose of controls is to ensure that only authorized program changes are made.

Background

Controls over systems software and application systems changes should be considered as part of the review of ERP general controls. However, the procedures used to control changes to programs are becoming increasingly application-dependent and nonstandardized. This is particularly true where there are online programming facilities. Where programs are written in-house, online programming facilities are common. Program changes may be on-line For applications where the input of transactions is offline, program changes may be online.

Typically, application programs will be cataloged in program libraries and stored on magnetic disk, in both source and object versions. Programmers will use terminals to access the source library and make program changes.

Control Procedures

- Use of program library software packages. Control over the cataloging of new or modified programs may be enhanced by the use of program library software. In general, these aids provide the following facilities:
  - Checking of authorized access to and changes of programs based on the use of passwords.
  - Maintenance of a file log that records program library access, program use, and changes.
  - Maintenance of an inventory of cataloged programs, identifications, and versions. Each program should have a version number that is increased by one each time the program is changed. The total number of source statements in each version may also be recorded.
  - Retention of specified prior versions.
  - Separate libraries for programs under development and in use (production programs).
  - Standard routines for transferring programs from the development to the production library, following management authorization.
  - Encryption (security coding) of sensitive programs.
  - Periodic or ad hoc hard copy printouts of program inventory, use, and changes.

Minicomputers

In minicomputer installations, control over changes to application programs is sometimes more difficult to achieve than in mainframe installations. This increased risk is due to lack of segregation of duties and easier facilities for changing programs. The potential control weaknesses are discussed below for two different situations.

compensating controls exist, we may not be able to rely on the computer's logic, and hence on the completeness and accuracy of processing.

Possible Compliance Tests

Confirm the adequacy of controls over access to the program library for both source and object versions. If a program library software package is used this may be done by testing the log of program changes for authorization.

Controls over Distributed Processing

Are there controls over distributed processing?

Purpose of the Controls

The purpose of controls is to ensure that the processing of data by a network of online computers is authorized, complete, and accurate.

Background

Distributed ERP processing, where a network of local computers or *intelligent terminals* is online to other computer installations, was discussed earlier in this chapter.

An important control consideration is whether programs can be modified locally. Programs issued centrally in object (machine) code are very difficult to modify locally. If the programs can be modified locally, the computer installation should be considered similar to any other stand-alone computer installation. There should, however, be some additional control procedures to reflect the fact that the computer is part of a network.

Control Procedures

- Adequate local editing procedures.
- Periodic reconciliation of data processed locally with that input for central processing.

- Periodic balancing of local and central data files.
- Issue of password-protected programs in object code only from a central library for local use.
- Procedures for central control of new programs or changes to programs that are stored or processed locally.
- Backup and recovery procedures. Terminal networks can be backed up effectively, although alternative telecommunications may not be feasible due to technical considerations or cost. If the network is disrupted but the computer installation is unaffected, it may be possible to send the input data physically to the installation for processing under batch control.

Compensating Controls and Significance of Weaknesses

Compensating controls may include:

- Local user controls over input and output for local ERP processing.
- Local controls over program changes.
- In the absence of such controls, the completeness and accuracy of processing may not be reliable.

Possible Compliance Tests

- Obtain a list of programs in the program libraries at local sites and review for the presence of unauthorized programs.
- Check that the local data file is reconciled to the central data file and that reconciling items are cleared.
- Check that errors detected by central validation programs are returned to the source location for correction.
- Carry out tests on local editing procedures.
- Review and test check client's reconciliations of data processed locally with that input for central processing.
- Confirm that backup and recovery procedures exist, appear adequate, and are tested.

Integrated Systems Controls

> *Are there procedures to control the transfer of data between inte-grated accounting systems?*

Purpose of the Controls

The purpose of controls is to ensure that the transfer of data and the re-sultant file updates are complete and accurate.

Background

The nature of integrated systems is discussed in Chapter 1.

Control Procedures

- Maintenance of an audit trail that records transfer of data between systems with respect to both control totals and individual items.
- Procedures to ensure that common standing data held on separate master files (e.g., product data held on both sales and inventory files) is the same at any point in time. If these procedures are not enforced, there may be mismatches that may result in differing acceptance, rejection, or suspension treatment.
- Accounting cut-off procedures to deal with the mismatches described above.
- Procedures to ensure that several user departments sharing a master file are all aware of changes made to common standing data.
- Where two or more files are simultaneously updated by online data entry, maintenance of separate control records that are balanced periodically.

Compensating Controls and Significance of Weaknesses

The main purpose of the above procedures is to prevent inconsistencies between the various parts of integrated accounting systems. If these controls are weak, the adequacy of the user controls over input and output for each accounting system, with special emphasis on cut-off at period-ends, will have to be considered. Cut-off errors may be compounded rather than highlighted in integrated systems. Instead of being exposed by different accounting procedures in separate systems, an error may be automatically repeated in more than one system.

Possible Compliance Tests

- Through discussion with user departments, check that:
  - Responsibilities for updating shared data are clearly defined.
  - Procedures exist and are followed to inform other users of changes to shared data.
  - Lack of coordination between users does not cause outstanding rejected data.
- Establish whether there is an adequate audit trail covering the transfer of data between accounting systems. Care should be taken not to duplicate testing of controls over input where one input item may be edited by one computer program, then used by other accounting systems.
- Review and test check client's reconciliations of the control records maintained for the various integrated files. Confirm that all necessary cut-off adjustments are made.

Database Controls

> *Are there database management system controls?*

Purpose of the Controls

The purpose of controls is to ensure that the database management system (DBMS) controls minimize the additional risks inherent in databases.

Background

The characteristics of database systems are described in Chapter 1.

Control Procedures

- Definition of each user's sub-schema that limits the user's ability to inquire, add, modify, or delete data. The sub-schemas should be defined after consultation with users and the database administration function. The DBMS should check every request for data against a table of security levels to ensure that the user, as identified by the password, is entitled to read the data and perform the functions requested.
- Inclusion in the DBMS of a utility program to check the coherence of the internal pointers and report inconsistencies (broken links).
- Inclusion in the DBMS of a check on every request for deletion of a data item to ensure that no dependent items will thus become inaccessible.
- Lock-out procedures that provide automatic prevention or detection by the DBMS of concurrent updating that may occur when two users attempt to access the same item simultaneously.
- Maintenance of transaction and recovery file logs both physically and logically separated from the database.
- Periodic scans of the database contents carried out by a program that accumulates individual records for agreement with a control record.

Compensating Controls and Significance of Weaknesses

Failure to restrict the processing capabilities of users and application programs leaves the database unprotected against inadvertent or unauthorized changes. Since they may not have an immediate impact on output, it is unlikely that the audit trail and associated user input/output reconciliation procedures would detect inadvertent changes. Tracing the source of an error in a database system is a complex task due to the logical interrelationships between data items. There is frequently no adequate compensating control in such a situation.

Failure to check the coherence of internal pointers may be compensated by strong user controls over database updating and reconciliation of control totals.

Possible Compliance Tests

- Establish that security levels for selected data items are appropriate, in conjunction with tests of the DBMS software or the data dictionary.
- Test the lock-out procedure by attempting simultaneous updates from adjacent terminals.
- Develop CAAT or use existing utility programs to test the coherence of internal pointers.

Is there a database administration function?

Purpose of the Controls

The purpose of controls is to ensure that there are adequate controls over the development and use of the database and appropriate liaison between users.

Background

As described in Chapter 1, one of the basic characteristics of a database system is the sharing of data between users. This sharing of data can produce user conflicts that must be arbitrated. Someone must provide a global perspective of the database's objectives so that a powerful user does not exercise undue influence.

Some clients will have both a DataBase Administrator (DBA) for technical aspects of the DBMS and a Data Administrator (DA) for administrative aspects of the DBMS; other clients will have either a DBA or DA. This function should be independent, not only of user departments, but also of ERP operations and programming. The DBA may have knowledge of the controls in operation, including passwords, and the capability of overriding these controls. The DBA function may be spread among several employees.

For a database installed in a minicomputer environment, there will normally be no separate full-time DBA. The function will usually be part of a senior systems analyst's responsibilities.

Control Procedures

- Appointment of a DBA responsible for:
  - Cost justification and planning.
  - Design of the database schema, including data content, data structure, and data relationships, as well as storage and access methods.
  - Development and implementation procedures for the DBMS.
  - Design and maintenance of the data dictionary/directory.
  - Specifying control procedures and documentation standards, including backup, dumping of copies, restart, and recovery.
  - Monitoring of database processing and reporting thereon to senior ERP management.
  - Liaison with users and auditors, including providing information on definitions, access paths, and security procedures.
  - Performance tuning.
  - Database testing to ensure integrity.
- Segregation of the duties of the DBA from:
  - Operational control of the day-to-day running of the database system.
  - Implementation and execution of security procedures.
  - Execution of restart and recovery procedures.
  - Design and coding of application programs.
  - Implementation of the database definitions.
  - Systems analysis and programming.
  - User department management.

Compensating Controls and Significance of Weaknesses

Compensating controls by individual users and the ERP department are needed if there is not an effective independent DBA function. The scope of audit procedures may need to be increased if there are no such controls.

Possible Compliance Tests

- Evaluate the degree to which the database administration function is independent of user departments and applications development, through discussion with senior personnel.
- Review documentary evidence of the DBA's work, such as procedure manuals, periodic reports, and notes on meetings.

Is a record of the database structure provided by the database management system or a data dictionary/directory?

Purpose of the Controls

The purpose of controls is to ensure that the database administration function, users, and ERP personnel are provided with an accurate picture of the structure of the database and the data elements that it contains. This should reduce the chance of systems analysis or programming errors and inappropriate reliance on programmed controls.

Background

As explained in Chapter 1, the logical structure of a database is defined by means of schema and sub-schema that are processed by the DBMS to enable application programs to process the data in the database. The schema represents the logical structure of the entire database, whereas each sub-schema contains only the data elements necessary for its application program.

Some organizations use a data dictionary/directory system to assist in documenting the database structure. It describes which data elements can be accessed and updated, by which users. It also shows the interrelationships between the various data elements. This can be an important control and audit tool. A data dictionary/directory system may be a written or computerized document. When computerized, it may be independent of the DBMS or may be integrated. If integrated, the DBMS and the data dictionary/directory will automatically be updated at the same time with the same data. This provides even better control.

Control Procedures

- Clear documentation of the database, including:
  - ○ Descriptions of each data element (data definitions) in language the users can understand.
  - ○ Source and format of the data elements.
  - ○ Application programs associated with each data element and record type.
  - ○ Interrelationships between data elements and record types.
  - ○ Edit and validation checks for each type of input.
  - ○ Users authorized to access or update data.
  - ○ Careful filing of information for ease of reference, with out-of-date information kept separately for historical reference.
  - ○ Confidential treatment of information, with access restricted on a need-to-know basis.
  - ○ Allocation of responsibility to the database administrator for ensuring the accuracy of information in the dictionary/directory.

Compensating Controls and Significance of Weaknesses

Inaccurate information may lead to programming errors or user reliance on nonexistent-programmed controls. These potential weaknesses may be compensated by user participation in system testing procedures. However, if programmers do not have an accurate view of the interrelationships between data items, they may introduce logic errors that may affect a different application. In this case, tests would probably not detect such errors. The DBA may have responsibility for this area. User controls over input and output should be relied upon in the absence of accurate documentation.

Failure to maintain the confidentiality of information may permit unauthorized access to and update of the database. Unauthorized access may be detected by a review of terminal access logs, while unauthorized updating may be exposed by a user input/output reconciliation, provided there is an adequate audit trail.

Possible Compliance Tests

- Review the types of information provided by the dictionary/directory. Check that security levels are appropriate for selected items.
- Use CAAT to reperform the edit and validation tests described in the dictionary/directory.
- Discuss with the database administration function the procedures for disclosing information to users and programmers, and the procedures for updating schema, sub-schema, and the data dictionary/directory.

SERVICE BUREAUS/OUTSOURCING

Bureaus may be independent companies or parts of other organizations such as banks or equipment manufacturers. The services provided by bureaus include renting computer time, timesharing, processing of software packages, and designing and processing of tailored (custom-built) application systems.

Additional control and audit considerations arise when a client outsources or uses a third party computer bureau or service center. The objectives of a review of internal control are the same as for in-house data processing, but the need for adequate procedures in certain control areas is increased. In addition, there may be some practical problems in attempting to apply the audit procedures suggested in this guide because of a bureau's reluctance to allow access to its computer, staff, and records.

In view of the continuing trend toward less costly and smaller computers used for in-house processing, there is likely to be less use of computer bureaus and more use of purchased packages on in-house computers. However, this has not been the case; thus far the trend has been outsourcing computer processing.

Practical Problems and Control Procedures

Historically, the majority of bureau applications have been offline batch-controlled systems. Therefore most clients that use bureaus have developed strong user controls. However, the use of online bureau systems, including in some cases international timesharing, is growing. This will increase the need to rely on ERP controls.

Since the client has no direct control over the procedures in operation at the bureau, the following matters should be agreed upon with the bureau:

- Liaison procedures. These should cover such matters as processing instructions and retention of source documents.
- Division of internal control duties. These should include correction and timely resubmission of rejections and input/output reconciliations.
- Systems and program documentation. This should always be available for both the client and the auditor. If the application has been tailor-made for a client, the client may possess the ownership rights and therefore have a full copy of the supporting documentation. On the other hand, if a package system is used, a bureau will not usually release copies of the detailed specifications to clients. The client should, however, have sufficient documentation to understand how to process input and output and to ensure that there are adequate controls overall.
- Backup for computer processing, data files, documentation, and staff.
- Restrictions over access to computer equipment, data files, and programs.
- ERP data control functions, including distribution of confidential output.

Since master files are not under the physical control of the client, there is an increased emphasis on in-house procedures for verifying the continuing authority, completeness, and accuracy of standing data.

Audit Planning

In determining our audit approach to bureau processing/outsourcing it is important to establish the following factors:

- The extent to which each bureau application relies on user or ERP controls. This will depend on the relative complexity of the system.

- The extent to which the client relies on the bureau's ERP general controls. This will depend partly on the client's reliance on ERP controls and partly on the client's dependence on the continuity of ERP processing at the bureau.
- Whether the bureau applications used are software packages, or designed and processed for clients only.
- Whether there is a report available, prepared by independent auditors, on either the software package used, or on the bureau's ERP general controls. This report may provide information on controls that can be relied upon to determine audit scope.

The following items are of interest in the review of a report prepared by independent auditors:

- Information on the period covered by the review.
- Information on the scope of audit work performed.
- Detailed descriptions of the systems and controls.
- Details of tests carried out.

Such reports usually include an opinion on whether the ERP and general controls were in conformity with prescribed procedures during the period covered by the review. The report will not give any opinion on the adequacy of bureau or user controls or on any client modifications to a standard package.

Auditors generally have no right of access to the premises or records of a computer bureau. Consequently, reviews of ERP general or application controls and use of CAAT at a bureau are dependent upon either the cooperation of bureau management, or a clause in the client's bureau contract that provides access.

Usually, audit obtains information about the bureau's controls by speaking with the client and examining the bureau contract. If additional evidence is required, audit should ask the client to arrange a visit to the bureau so that controls can be evaluated. In some cases, this step may involve the signing of a *nondisclosure agreement* with the bureau.

Audit should report any recommendations from their assessment of controls to their clients. Audit should also encourage their organization to submit extracts of audit reports to the bureau.

SUMMARY OF CONTROL QUESTIONS

Application Controls by Users

- *Controls over input.*
  Are there user controls over the preparation and approval of transactions?
  Does the user control input?
- *Controls over standing data.*
  Are there user controls over changes to standing data on master files and look-up tables?
  Are there user controls over the continuing completeness and accuracy of standing data on master files and look-up tables?
- *Controls over rejections and suspense items.*
  Are there user controls over rejected transactions?

  Does the user control suspense items?
- *Controls over output.*
  Are there user controls over output?

Application Controls by Data Control Group

- *Controls over input.*
  Does the data control group control input?
- *Controls over output.*
  Are there control procedures within the data control group concerning review and distribution of output?

Application Controls by ERP Processing

- *Controls over input.*

  Are there controls over key transcription?
  Is there editing and validation of input?
- *Controls over suspense items.*
  Are there data processing controls over suspense items?
- *Controls over processing.*
  Are data processing controls used to balance the transaction and master files?
  Is there an adequate audit trail?

General Controls

- *Segregation of duties and security.*
  Is there segregation of duties within the data processing function?
  Are there controls which restrict unauthorized physical access to the computer room, terminals, tape and disk files, and systems and programming documentation?

- *Controls over ERP systems software.*
  Are there controls over changes to ERP systems software?

- *Controls over operations.*

  Are there procedures to minimize the risk that unauthorized jobs and programs are run?
  Are there controls that ensure the use of the correct tape and disk files?
  Is there supervision of computer operations staff for all shifts?

- *Controls over continuity of processing.*
  Are there procedures to prevent a disaster affecting the ERP function from causing a major disruption to the information flow or a loss of accounting control?
  Is the documentation of the ERP function adequate to ensure that the client can continue in operation if important ERP staff left its employment?

- *Controls over application systems development.*

  Is there user involvement in the development of new application systems and modifications to existing systems?
  Are there testing procedures for new systems and modifications to existing systems?
  Are there implementation procedures for new systems and modifications to existing systems?

Additional Controls for Advanced ERP Systems

- *Controls over online input.*

  Are there controls to restrict online terminal use to authorized persons?
  Is there balancing of control totals for online input?
  Is there an adequate audit trail of individual items entered for processing using online terminals?

- *Recovery and restart procedures for online systems.*
  Are there recovery and restart procedures in the event of online transmission or processing failure?
- *Controls over online program changes.*
  Are there controls over online program changes?
- *Controls over distributed processing.*
  Are there controls over distributed processing?
- *Integrated system controls.*
  Are there procedures to control the transfer of data between integrated accounting systems?
- *Database controls.*
  Are there database management system controls?
  Is there a database administration function?
  Is a record of the database structure provided by the database management system or a data dictionary/directory?

6

SAP Overview and Basis Component Review

SAP R/3 is one of the most complex ERP systems, and auditing in this environment can prove to be quite a challenge to the auditor. Although SAP R/3 has been around for quite some time, the knowledge base regarding audits in this environment is still evolving.

An audit can be performed for various reasons based on the organizational need. It could be a pre-implementation or a post-implementation audit or it could be the ongoing audit performed to monitor system integrity or to test controls based upon management's control objectives.

SAP R/3 ORGANIZATIONAL MODEL

One of the first challenges an auditor faces is to determine the scope of the audit. To fully understand scope one needs to understand the SAP R/3 organizational hierarchy, also known as the organizational model. Although the organizational model can be flexible and complex, once configured, it has permanent impact on the organization. The organizational model is designed and configured in each module and, based on this design, the system tables are set up accordingly.

System

At the very top level of the organizational model is the system, or instance. A system is a stand-alone set of hardware and one instance of the SAP R/3 database. A system usually has a single database server however, a system can have several application servers each running the SAP R/3 software. In a typical SAP R/3 landscape, there are three systems: the development system (DEV), the quality assurance system (QAS), and the production system (PRD). Each system has its own functionality and its own purpose for existence in the SAP R/3 environment.

Configuration is usually done in DEV; all the testing is performed in QAS, and the production or live data and transactions are carried out in PRD. Unless it is a pre-implementation review, the auditor can usually limit the audit to the production system. In large implementations, each system resides in its own environment, and data transfer between the systems is controlled. There can be multiple PRD systems in an organization, and each PRD system then will most likely require its own audit.

Client

The next level in the SAP R/3 organizational model is the client. Technically speaking, a client is a logical separation of the database. There are some default clients in the SAP R/3 system that are recommended by SAP and, typically, one production client. The data of one client cannot be accessed by another client in the same system because most of the data reside in "client-dependent" tables or are specific to that particular client. Some data, however, are managed at the system level and shared by all clients in the system, and these reside in "client-independent" tables. Because of the nature of the system setup, each client usually requires its own separate audit.

The three default clients seen in a typical system are clients 000, 001, and 066. Like the three SAP R/3 systems in the landscape, each client has its own functionality. The client 000 includes base parameters for all applications, standard settings, and configurations for controls and, therefore, is a special client for the system. It contains the client-independent settings.

Client 001 is a copy of the client 000 and, once configured and customized, its settings are client-dependent. This is the client that is used to set up or copy other clients in the system.

Client 066 is reserved by SAP and is used for troubleshooting. It is also called the Early Watch client.

In addition, another client exists in the system and is typically the production client. In rare instances, one might find more or fewer than the four clients. A system administrator must justify to an auditor a specific reason for deviating from the SAP recommended setup. System integrity may be compromised with the existence of each additional client other than the ones mentioned above.

Chart of Accounts

Typically, the account number in a standard general ledger chart of accounts denotes all the organizational and account information. Therefore, in a large organization, it is customary to see charts of accounts that contain a large number of digits. Because in SAP R/3, organizational information such as the company code resides separately, the account numbers may not contain a large number of digits.

The chart of accounts resides higher than the company code that allows different companies within an organization to use the exact same chart of accounts. The same chart of accounts may be maintained in different languages.

Company Code

Company code is the unit within the organizational model that contains the general ledger. It is typically a legal entity and an accounting entity for which a balanced set of financial statements are produced.

There are other components in the organizational model that are configured at the module level and that an auditor needs to understand in order to set up the scope of the audit.

A typical SAP R/3 review is performed in two phases. One phase is a review of the technical aspect of the system, or the SAP R/3 Basis Component; the other phase is a review of the business processes or cycles, such as expenditure or revenue. Because of the complexity and extremely technical nature of the system, SAP R/3 reviews require a person who understands this environment and is trained to perform such reviews.

SAP R/3 Authorization Concept

Fundamental to SAP R/3 security is the *Authorization Concept*. To understand SAP R/3 security, it is necessary to thoroughly understand the authorization concept. This concept allows the assignment of broad or finely defined authorizations or permissions for system access. Several authorizations may be required in SAP R/3 to perform a task such as creating a material master record. Based on the design, these authorizations can be limited to: (1) access to the transaction code (TCODE) to create material master, (2) access to the specific material, and (3) authorization to work in a particular plant in the system.

Authorization Object

The authorization object can best be described as locks that limit access to SAP R/3 system objects such as programs, TCODES, data entry screens, and so forth. Depending on the SAP R/3 version, there are approximately 800 standard authorizations. There can be 10 fields in an authorization object; however, all 10 fields are not used in all objects. The most common field in an authorization object is the activity field. These are predefined activity codes that reside in a table named TACT. Examples of this activity are "01"—create or generate, "02"—change, "03"—read, "04"—print or edit message, "06"—delete. The next most common field is an organization field, such as a company code or plant.

Authorization objects are classified and cataloged in the system based on functionality such as FI (Financial Accounting) or HR (Human Resources). These classifications are called object classes.

Developers and programmers can create new authorization objects through the developers' workbench, which is called ABAP Workbench in SAP R/3. ABAP/4 is a 4GL (fourth-generation programming language) that was used to develop all SAP R/3 applications. It stands for Advanced Business Application Programming Language.

Authorizations

Authorizations are the keys that can open the authorization objects and contain the specific information for field values. For instance, an authorization can contain a specific set of values for one or all the fields of a particular authorization object. If a field is not restricted, an authorization will have a "*" as a field value, which means that a particular field does not have any restrictions.

An example of an authorization is as follows:

Field	Value
ACTVT (Activity)	01
BUKRS (Company Code)	0010

This particular authorization will grant users access to create for company code 0010 the specific object that is being locked by the authorization object such as a purchase order.

The following authorization will grant total access to all activities for all company codes:

Field	Value
ACTVT (Activity)	*
BUKRS (Company Code)	*

Profiles or Activity Group

Authorizations are assigned not directly to a user but to authorization profiles. There are simple profiles that can contain up to 150 authorizations. Two or more simple profiles are then assigned to a composite profile. SAP R/3 has standard composite profiles that are grouped together for functionality. For instance, a profile for an accounts payable accountant will contain all the authorizations to perform that job function. The most talked about profile in SAP R/3 is SAP_ALL. This profile contains all the standard authorizations with all field values with "*" and grants unlimited access to the system.

User Master Record

User master records contain specific information regarding the user such as dialog, system, and so forth. They also contain other user information, such as address, valid dates, user group, and most importantly, the profile information for that particular user.

There are four default users SAP R/3 users. These are SAP*, CPIC, DDIC, and EARLYWATCH.

SAP* is the default system super user with SAP_ALL profiles. When a new client is created in a SAP system, a SAP* account is created by default. The CPIC or Common Programming Interface Communication user is used for program-to-program communication within the R/3 system.

User DDIC is the ABAB/4 data dictionary maintenance and software logistics user. This user is used for certain installation and setup tasks and should not be deleted.

Authorization Checks

How does SAP R/3 know how to check for authorizations? All this information is hard coded to the programs or ABAPs via AUTHORITY-CHECK statements. Since most SAP R/3 ABAPs contain AUTHORITY-CHECK statements, it is a good policy for an organization to have standards that include authority check statements in customized programs.

SAP R/3 BASIS COMPONENT REVIEW

A SAP R/3 Basis Component review is a sanity check for the implemented system and must be performed after an implementation or upgrade and at least annually thereafter. One can perform a very extensive Basis Component review or a fairly high level review. Here, we will discuss performing a high-level Basis Component review.

Basis Component Review

What is the Basis Component? Basis Component is an integral part of the SAP R/3 system and is the layer in which all the system functionality resides. Each R/3 system has its own Basis Component, which is shared by all clients and modules in the system. The Basis Component is ubiquitous and is incorporated throughout the R/3 system. Basis Component controls system analysis and customization; structures and control; processing: programming; data and storage; and operations and control.

Below, we discuss some of the steps that are recommended in performing a Basis Component Review.

Run the RSUSR003 Report

This is a report I call the "System Pulse" report. You can review this report and in a minute get the pulse of the system that is being reviewed. It provides some very high-level information about the SAP R/3 system.

This report has two sections. The first section shows some very high-level system parameters, and the second section details the clients in the system and the status of each of the default user accounts that are created in each client.

Some of the more significant of these parameters are discussed below:

Parameter: login/disable_multi_gui_login   "0"

To disable multiple logons with the same user account, set this to "1."

Parameter: login/failed_user_auto_unlock   "0"

To enable automatic unlock of locked user at midnight, set this parameter to "1." The recommended setting is "0."

Parameter: login/fails_to_session_end   "3"

Number of invalid login attempts until the SAP R/3 session ends.

The recommended setting is "3."

Parameter: login/fails_to_user_lock   "6"

Number of invalid login attempts until user lock.

The recommended setting is "3."

Parameter: login/min_password_lng   "6"

Minimum password length. The recommended setting is at least "5."

Parameter: login/multi_login_users   ""

This lists the users who are allowed multiple R/3 session login.

Parameter: login/no_automatic_user_sapstar   "0"

This setting allows the regeneration of the user SAP* if accidentally deleted. The recommended setting is "1."

Parameter: login/password_expiration_time   "90"

The number of days until the password must be changed.

The next part of this report lists the clients in the system and the status of the default passwords. If the passwords have not been changed, this report will highlight that account in red along with the password. The only allowable exception is the SAPCPIC account with the password ADMIN. This password is hard-coded in several

R/3ABAPs, and changing this could make the system act in an unpredictable manner. Careful consideration should be given before changing the SAPCPIC password.

Reviewing the RSPARAM Report

In addition to the parameters listed above, an auditor should also review the RSPARAM report. This report lists the system parameters with the default values and the changed values. Although some of these are technical parameters, the parameters listed in the RSUSR003 report also appear in this report in more detail, with default and changed values.

Reviewing the USR40 Table for Entries

The list of prohibited user passwords should be included in this table. Some organizations go to extreme lengths and populate this table with the entire dictionary. At the minimum, this table should contain some common entries, such as the months, days of the week, and the organization's name. An example is shown in Exhibit 6.1.

> Method of Execution: *SE16 (Data Browser)* → *Press Enter* →
> *Enter 'USR40' in the Table field* → *Press Enter* → *Make Required*
> *Entries* → *Press F8 (Execute)*

Reviewing the Company Codes for Productive Flags

During implementation, certain system flags are not set for a production environment. One of these flags is the productive flag for company codes. Not setting this flag allows one to "undo" transactions made to the system with deletion programs. Setting this flag to productive protects audit trails and should be checked. To check for productive status, execute transaction OBR3 and review the "Productive" column to see if there are check marks by the company codes (see Exhibit 6.2).

> Method of Execution: *OBR3 (Maintain Table T001-Company*
> *Codes)* → *Press Enter*

Exhibit 6.1   Table USR40 Select Entries

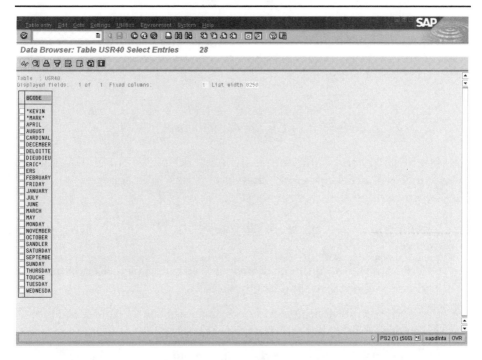

Exhibit 6.2   Productive Indicator Overview

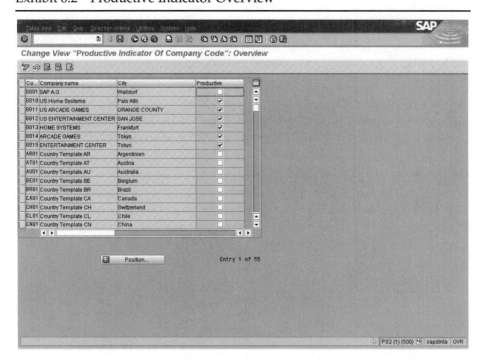

Reviewing to See if the System Is Locked

Once configuration is complete and the system is in the productive stage, it should be locked to prevent inadvertent changes from being made. The screen to make these changes can be accessed via transaction code SCC4 (see Exhibit 6.3).

> Menu Path: *Menu → SAP Menu → Tools → Administration → Client Administration → Client Maintenance (SCC4)*

Highlight each client one at a time and press enter. The screen shown in Exhibit 6.4 appears. This screen has four separate sections. The recommended settings for these sections are:

Changes and transports for client-specific objects: "No changes allowed"

Client-independent object settings: "No changes to Repository and cross-client Customizing objects"

Protection: Client copier and comparison tool: "Protection level 2: No overriding, no external availability"

Restrictions: "Currently locked due to client copy" should be checked.

Reviewing Users with SAP_ALL Profile

The most important transaction code that an auditor requires in an R/3 system is the report RSUSR002 or transaction SUIM (User Information System. This report is used for various audit queries about users, profiles, and authorizations. Using this report for queries is quite tricky and one needs to know how to use it effectively. SAP R/3 usually does not check for invalid input parameters; therefore, it is necessary to pay particular attention when using this query tool.

There are several ways to access this tool. The first method is via transaction SA38. Once in the SA38 screen, type RSUSR002 as program name and you should get the screen shown in Exhibit 6.5.

> Using transaction SUIM: *SUIM → User → Users by complex selection criteria → Click on Users by complex selection criteria and hit execute.*

Exhibit 6.3   Display View "Clients": Overview

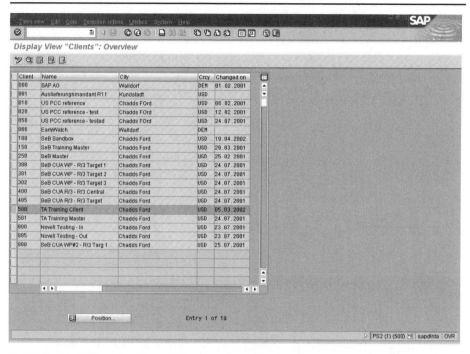

Exhibit 6.4   Display View "Clients": Details

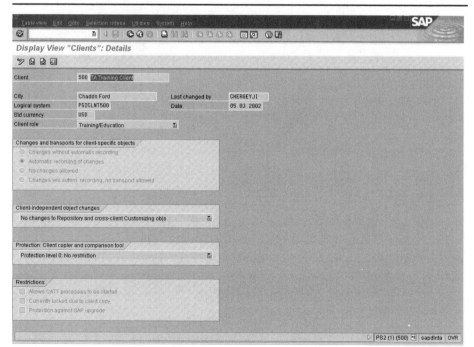

Exhibit 6.5   RSUSR002 Screen

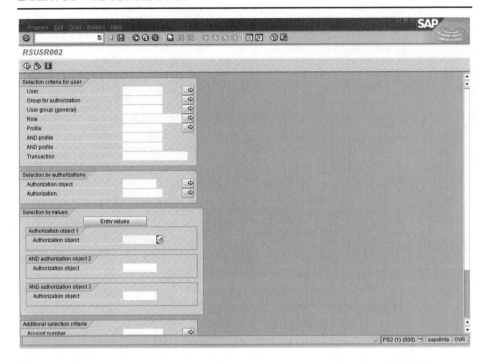

Menu Path: *Tools → Administration → User Maintenance → Information System → User → Users by complex selection criteria → Double Click on: S_BCE_68001400 - Users by complex selection criteria*

To get a list of users with SAP_ALL access, enter SAP_ALL in the profile box and click execute. Typically, very few users should have this level of open access. The auditor should review the user list with management to ensure that no unauthorized user has this access.

Securing User SAP*

The SAP system is delivered with a default super user, SAP*. The default password for this account is well known.

At installation, a user master record is defined for SAP*; however, SAP* is programmed into the system and does not need a user master record. If the user master record is deleted, it regenerates itself with a well-known password.

SAP* should be deactivated using the following steps:

1. A new password should be assigned to SAP*.

2. All profiles should be deleted from the SAP* user master record so that SAP* has no authorizations.

3. SAP* should be assigned to the user group SUPER to prevent easy deletion or modification of its user master record.

4. The SAP* user ID should also be locked, once the other actions above have been completed (the order is important).

5. The special attributes of the user ID SAP* should be deactivated. This can be done by changing the default value 0 to 1 for the system profile parameter login/no_automatic_user_sap*.

Reviewing the List of Inactive Users

In a large organization, over time the user list may come to contain several terminated users, inactive users, or users who have never logged in. In some cases, the list of inactive users can grow to a significant number. An auditor should review user access logs and ensure that the user list contains active users only. This can be done by reviewing the table USR02, shown in Exhibit 6.6.

Exhibit 6.6   Table USR02 Select Fields

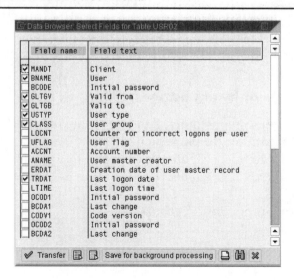

Menu Path: *Execute Transaction Code SE16 (Data Browser) →*
Enter 'USR02' in the Table field → Go to Settings → List Format
→ Choose Fields → Click Transfer Button → Press F8 (Execute)

Review the TRDAT or last logon field for current dates. If this field
has all zeroes, then the user has never logged in to the system.

A good user maintenance procedure is to lock all terminated users
and then assign them to a terminated user group. After a period of time
(between two to three years), these users should be removed from the
system.

Reviewing the Security of Custom ABAPs

One of the methods used by SAP to control the execution of programs
is to establish authorization groups and assign programs to these
groups. A group's access to critical programs can be restricted by assigning it to a restrictive program authorization group. As a rule, all
custom programs should be assigned to authorization groups. SAP's
recommended naming methodology requires all custom programs to
be named with the initial letter Y or Z.

Method of Execution: *SE16 (Data Browser) → Press Enter →*
Enter 'TRDIR' in the Table field → Press Enter → Enter Y* or Z*
in the name field → Press F8 (Execute)

Any program with entry in the SECU column is assigned to an authorization group. While this is one way of securing custom programs,
there are several other ways to secure them, such as assigning them custom transaction codes and securing these transaction codes.

Reviewing the Security of Custom Tables

Like custom programs, customized tables are also secured by assigning
them to authorization groups, which typically have names beginning
with a Y or Z. To do this, execute the query as shown in the customized
program tested above. The table name to view is TDDAT and the field
is CCLASS. Those tables with &NC& in the CCLASS column are not
assigned to any authorization group.

Checking for Users Who Have Program Execution Access

Executing queries for "Who has access to" critical functionality is a complicated task in a R/3 environment. Since transaction codes are paired with authorization objects and these objects require specific authorizations, an auditor has to have a good understanding of the system in order to get the query parameters, as well as a good understanding of how to use the RSUSR002 report.

A limitation of this report is that it can check only three parameters at a time. For example, if a transaction code is associated with six authorization objects that all have authorization values, the query needs to be performed in three steps. First, the transaction code and two authorization objects; next, three other authorization objects; then finally, the last authorization object. The query results are saved in three separate spreadsheets or tables, and the common user records in all three tables are the users with the ability to perform a specific task. You can use an audit tool like ACL or Microsoft access to combine and extract the results of the queries.

The procedure for checking for users who have Program Execution Access is shown in Exhibits 6.7–6.10. The steps to follow are:

Step 1: *Execute Transaction Code SE16 → Enter 'USOBT' in the Table Field → Enter 'SA38' in the Name field → Press F8 (Execute)*

Step 2: *Execute RSUSR002 report (Menu Path mentioned previously) → Enter Required Authorization Objects in the fields (from table USOBT) → Press Enter → Enter the Required Activity fields (from table USOBT) → Press F8 (Execute)*

Users with Access to Maintaining Critical/Custom tables

Tables are a critical component of the SAP R/3 system because they contain controlling information for the system as well as transactions entered by users. In particular, changes to client-independent tables that contain global definition data can have unexpected side effects, as the changes affect all clients in a SAP system. Both client-dependent and client-independent tables control how the system functions, and inadvertent or unauthorized changes to them could have serious consequences. Therefore, access to table maintenance should be restricted.

Exhibit 6.7   Execute Transaction Code SE16

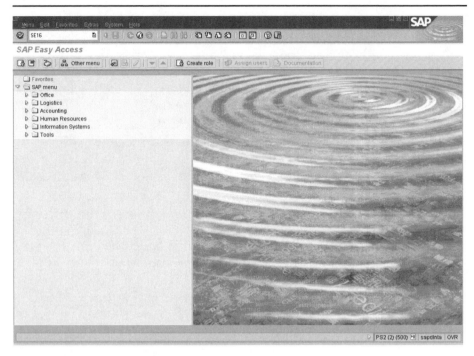

Exhibit 6.8   Enter USOBT

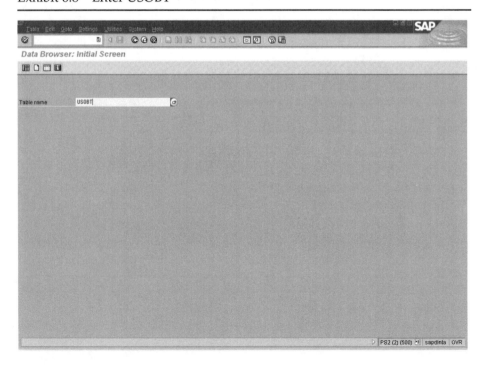

Exhibit 6.9   Enter SA38

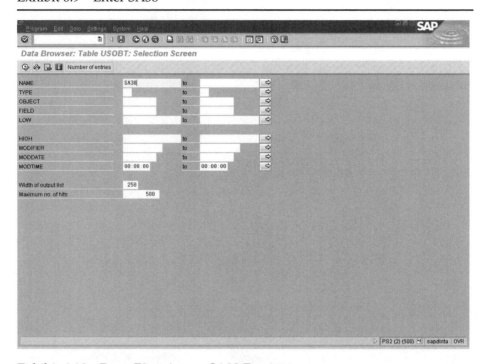

Exhibit 6.10   Press F8 to Access SA38 Entries

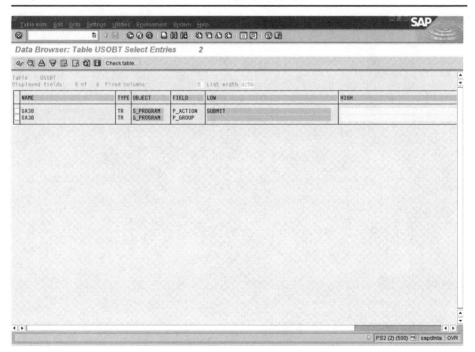

The client-independent tables are secured by authorization object S_TABU_CLI and the client-dependent tables are secured by S_TABU_DIS.

The procedure to check for users who have access to Maintaining Criticial/Custom tables consists of the following two steps (see Exhibits 6.11–6.13).

Step 1: *Execute Transaction Code SE16 → Enter 'USOBT' in the Table Field → Enter 'SM31 the Name field → Press F8 (Execute)*

Step 2: *Execute RSUSR002 report (Menu Path mentioned previously) → Enter Required Authorization Objects in the fields (from table USOBT) → Press Enter → Enter the Required Activity fields (from table USOBT) → Press F8 (Execute)*

Exhibit 6.11   Enter SM31

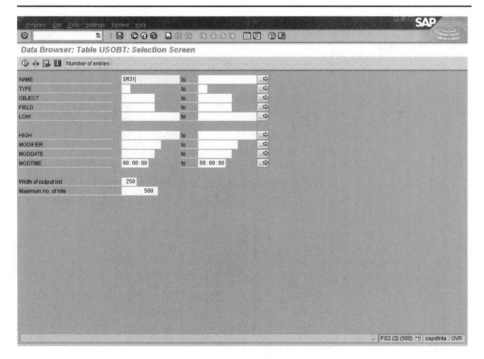

Exhibit 6.12   Press F8 to Access SM31 Entries

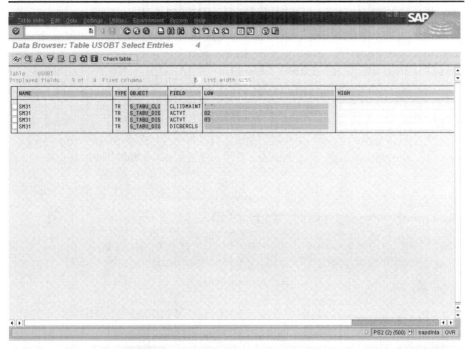

Exhibit 6.13   RSUSR002 Report

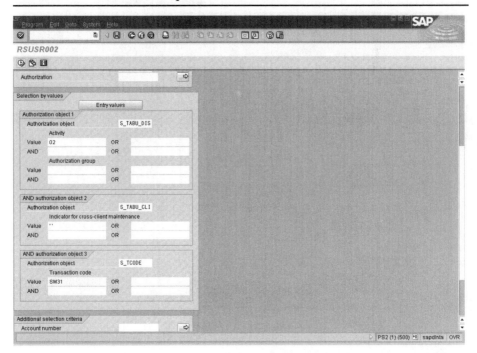

Reviewing the System for Locking Critical Transaction Codes

There are several transaction codes in the system that are extremely powerful and rarely used once a system is in production. An organization should determine which of these transaction codes are "critical" and lock these transactions. Execute transaction SM01 to view or change locked transaction codes. The locked transaction codes have a check mark in the box in the "locked" box (see Exhibit 6.14).

Menu Path: *Menu → SAP Menu → Tools → Administration → Administration → Transaction Code Administration (SM01)*

Users with Access to User Maintenance

User maintenance is one of the most critical functions within SAP R/3 and, therefore, this functionality should be highly restricted.The proce-

Exhibit 6.14   Transaction Codes: Lock/Unlock

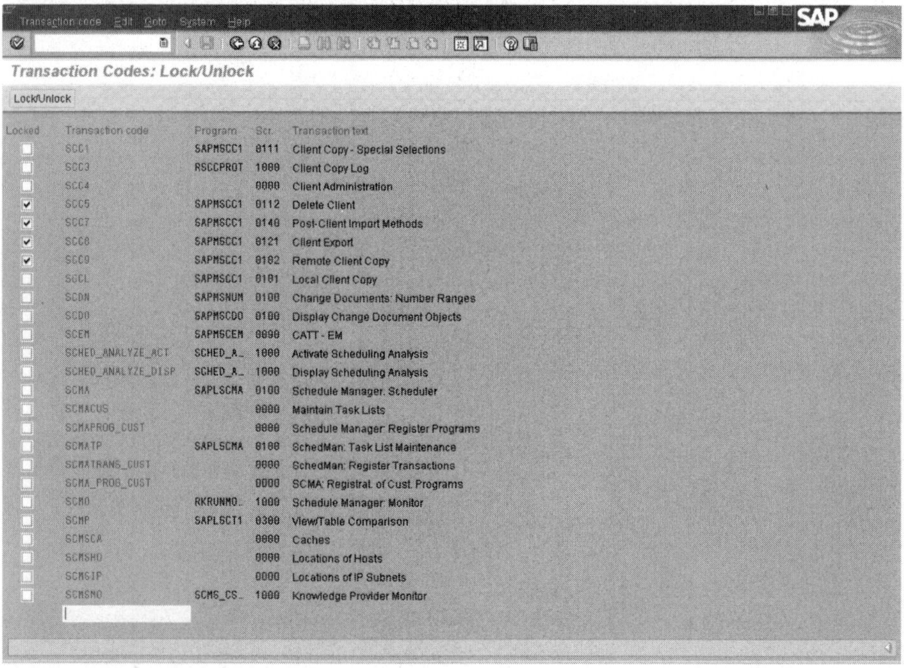

dure to check for users with access to User Maintenance is described below and shown in Exhibits 6.15–6.17:

> Step 1: *Execute Transaction Code SE16 → Enter 'USOBT' in the Table Field → Enter 'SU01' in the Name field → Press F8 (Execute)*

> Step 2: *Execute RSUSR002 report (Menu Path mentioned previously) → Enter Required Authorization Objects in the fields (from table USOBT) → Press Enter → Enter the Required Activity fields (from table USOBT) → Press F8 (Execute)*

These steps represent a very high level review of the Basis Component. This is an excellent starting point for conducting an SAP audit.

Exhibit 6.15   Enter SU01

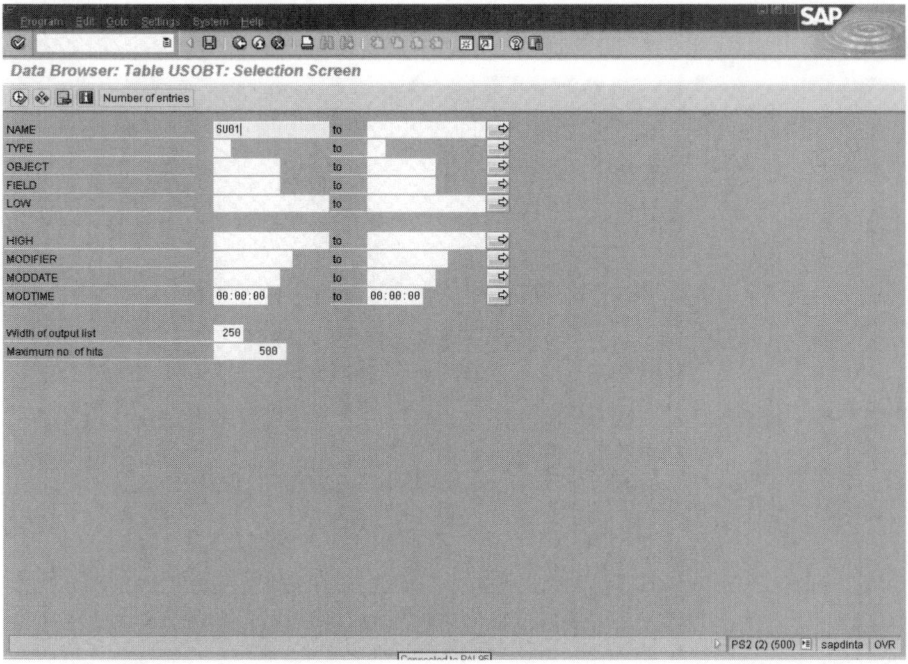

Exhibit 6.16　Press F8 to Access SU01 Entries

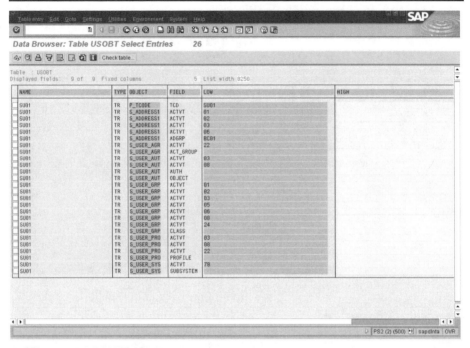

Exhibit 6.17　RSUSR002 Report

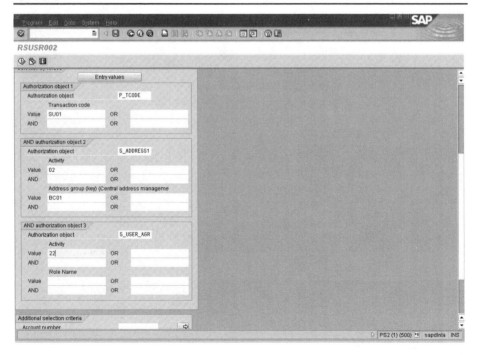

Index